THE
MAGIC
OF NOT FITTING IN
A Story of Family Empowerment
in Changing Times

TORY LENORMAND

The Magic Of Not Fitting In: A Story of Family Empowerment in Changing Times
Copyright©2024 by Tory Lenormand, All rights reserved.

No part of this publication may be used or reproduced, stored in a retrieval system, or transmitted in any form or by any means—electronic, mechanical, photocopying, recording, or otherwise—without the prior written permission of the author. No portion of this book may be reproduced, copied, distributed or adapted in any way, with the exception of certain activities permitted by applicable copyright laws, such as brief quotations in the context of a review or academic work. For permission to publish, distribute or otherwise reproduce this work, please contact the author at tory@geminidirections.co.uk.

The views expressed in this work are solely those of the author. The author of this book does not dispense medical advice or prescribe the use of any technique as a form of treatment for physical, emotional, or medical matters without considering personal medical advice. The intent of the author is only to offer information of a general nature to support you in your quest for balance and wellbeing. In the event you use any of the information in this book, as is your right, the author and publisher assume no responsibility for your actions.

With consideration to the dynamic nature of the internet, any web addresses or links contained in this book may have changed since publication and may no longer be valid.

First published in the United Kingdom by Fae Blood Publications, 2024 faebloodpublications.com.au

Editing: Ruth Fae, Fae Blood Publications
Graphic Design: Kristina Conatser, Captured By KC Designs
Illustrations by: Aisha Haider

ISBN: 978-1-7637813-0-6

British Library Cataloguing-in-Publication Data A catalogue record for this book is available from the British Library.

This memoir is based on the author's recollections of events. In some cases, names, details, and events have been changed, withheld, condensed, or combined to protect the privacy of individuals. Any resemblance to actual persons, living or dead, outside of the author's experiences is coincidental.

Disclaimer

I AM A BELIEVER in the phrase attributed to Anglo-Irish statesman and philosopher Edmund Burke,

> *"The only thing necessary for the triumph of evil is for good men to do nothing."*

The contents of my book are my reflections on experiences I have had with our systems of Education, Health, and Justice in the United Kingdom and Guernsey. My conclusions are drawn from all of these experiences which include working and living in both geographical areas. I've never been asked not to speak about them to a wider audience. The purpose of writing this book is to:

- Offer insight, from a parental perspective, to those who are reviewing educational practices.

- Offer community to those who have shared our experiences and feel unheard or excluded from the communities they belonged to.

- Raise awareness of why "School Refusal" is more than just a headline, but a call to action from our children and many of their teachers.

I invite you to take what you need, and leave what you don't. But hear the problem because it's not going away—and our children's voices are getting louder.

"The fact is that given the challenges we face, education doesn't need to be reformed—it needs to be transformed. The key to this transformation is not to standardise education, but to personalise it, to build achievement on discovering the individual talents of each child, to put students in an environment where they want to learn and where they can naturally discover their true passions."

— **Sir Ken Robinson,** *The Element: How Finding Your Passion Changes Everything* (Robinson 2009)

*To Yves, who bore this firmly beside me,
my best friend and comfiest rock.*

*To George, for his grace as I practised being a mum and
his understanding as I changed all I thought I knew.*

To the wise women of Guernsey who witnessed this transition.

To Cacao, for refilling my cup in every sense.

*And to William, who initiated the change he
wanted to see in this world.*

Contents

Part I. Introduction	1
Part II. Early Challenges	15
Part III. A New Beginning	93
Part IV. Life on the Road	99
Part V. Big Dreams and Aspirations	107
Part VI. Settling and Growth	113
Part VII. Conclusion	121
Epilogue	133
References	139
Acknowledgements	147
About the Author	149

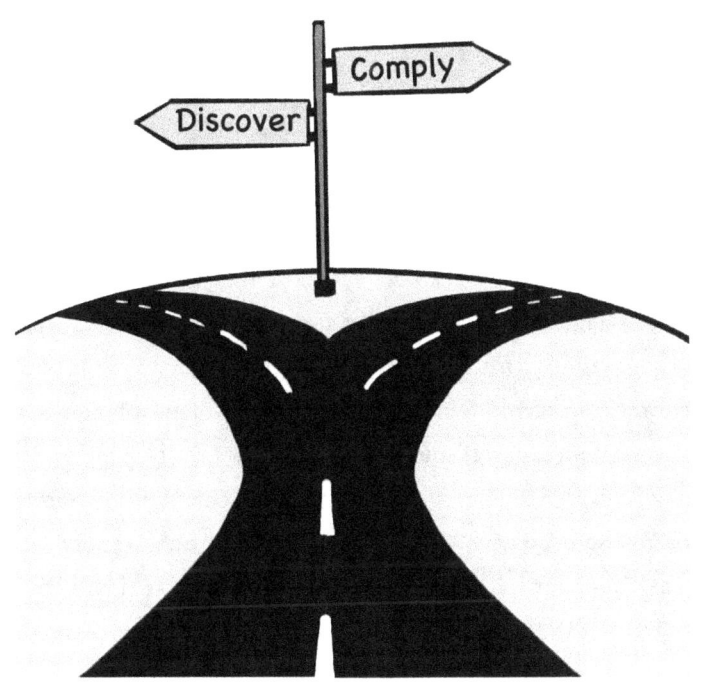

Part I. Introduction

OUR FAMILY HAS UNDERGONE a transformation, reshaping itself because I started to question the meanings of "Family" and "Education." When our youngest son was defined as having special educational needs, I did not really know what that meant at the time, beyond it qualifying him for help.

Education - *noun*

- the process of receiving or giving systematic instruction, especially at a school or university." A course of education"

Family - *noun*

- a group of one or more parents and their children living together as a unit."The family lived in a large house with a lot of land."

Defining education as a process of "systemic instruction at a school or university" gives weight to the idea of "system" over "discovery." However, the weight we have come to attribute to this "system" over any idea of discovery is disproportionate. In trying to meet standardisation (ticking all the boxes), the needs of the systems missed the humanity in my family. The way we worked and financially supported ourselves was threatened, all in the name of serving a system in a recognised way. As we collapsed under the weight of the demands, I began to ask questions. I found these questions to be so unwelcome that our family came under threat at a time when our eldest son was transitioning into adulthood, our workspaces were crumbling, and our youngest son desperately struggled on.

At this key point, we chose to reimagine what education looked like and to challenge our own thoughts and beliefs. We transformed, to aim for thriving rather than surviving. Our way reimagines our Education, our Health, and our sense of Justice and Community.

There are many ways to look at the challenges each of us face in our day-to-day lives. We can look for meaning and definition in a book or online, or we can look inside ourselves for what feels right for us. The latter sounds a little vague but it is, ultimately, how I feel about something that has come to matter very much to me. As we continue to be the change in our own lives, we hope to inspire you to embrace the unknown and discover the incredible possibilities that lie beyond our comfort zones.

This is our journey of a mum, a dad, two sons, an Autism Diagnosis, school, and a whole lot of questions about trying to "fit in."

If you want to explore some of the questions we have asked, you can find even more information in the Epilogue: Looking Forward

Who Are We?

Tory: Sat on the floor beside my mum's armchair, in the middle floor lounge of our town house, Mum leaned down towards me holding a "Peter and Jane" book. I was staring at the page when the penny dropped… I could read! Tears sprang to my eyes. I felt so proud that I had learned to read, and still recall the smile on Mum's face, a smile that reached deep in her eyes and crinkled there. The words flowed from me and she knew I understood. This gift she gave me through her teaching and nurturing was so special and precious. Able to read fluently before I started school, I still enjoy the peace and learning that comes from a good book.

My sister was born two days before my third birthday, and we moved from that town house soon after.

At "play school" (England's kindergarten), I remember cutting out shapes in potatoes, dipping them in paint, and creating art on a large piece of paper pinned to an easel. And as I played next to a stack of canoes, I wondered what it would be like to be at sea in a canoe, or to be on the train that passed us on the nearby track. It was a time of imagination and creative play that was about being in the moment.

Fast forward and by the time I was twelve, I realised my parents were dog-tired. They both worked hard, and my dad worked shifts that were ever-changing. I experienced stressed-out parents who, as shift-workers, passed like ships in the night. Add to that all the volunteer work my parents engaged in, plus their community support roles and raising my sister and I, and I now understand the stress. For a long time, I worried that they would split up. Divorce was happening all around me, with my friends' parents and in our social groups. In hindsight, I can see that in the late 1970s/early 1980s, the expectations upon my parents, the sudden hike in cost of living, and the rise of their mortgage repayments due to crippling interest rates, were enough to cause levels of insurmountable stress. It's understandable that so many people were broken—broken homes, broken financially, and broken morale.

In 2023, as I write this, they are firmly together having strived to be so. A similar economic climate is shrouding us and I find myself watching families manage increasing tides of pressure with limited signs of reprieve.

I remember feeling very confused as a twelve-year-old child. Only a few years earlier my parents had been encouraged to purchase property, to own their own home. I think I was about seven when we moved into our house. It was a big deal to be the first people in their family to own their house. Thanks to Margaret Thatcher and the drive for home ownership across England, this became a significant "success" marker for many people, including my parents.

I sensed this as the call of their time. It also drove the "education" I received from my home environment: buying a house was the ultimate goal. And to get to this coveted position of home ownership, you needed regular and risk-free work, with as little chance as possible of losing your job. A steady income enabled you to prove to a bank that you could afford a mortgage; regular and safe employment was the way to reach that goal. It enabled you to apply for the high levels of debt required to afford a space to live in, a home to call your own. But was this just a big trap?

The systems we live in feed these beliefs. I may go as far as to say they actively craft them. When I was a child, I learned that my start in adult life depended on doing well at school. It all started at school—this was the only way to get a good job, have a reliable income, and be able to buy a house. On reflection, it is both understandable and equally amazing how completely my parents embodied this. They felt "successful" because they bought their own home, which was only possible because they worked hard and sacrificed every day.

My parents were also supportive extracurricular parents. Valuing the rounded development that came with sporting achievement outside of school, they volunteered their time as gymnastic coaches to my sister and me, along with about a hundred other young children. They knocked themselves out being all they could be at work and home.

They maintained this for years and my father still serves his community in a voluntary capacity. To them, community contribution aids everyone, and also means you belong. But it took its toll. Exhausted parents can make for a fractious home environment.

My dad, a local police officer, worked a lot of overtime and was, on occasion, sent away to support police services in other areas. If that was not enough, people also knocked on our door looking for support. He never stopped working. In all fairness, he explained to me that, the majority of the time, he loved it, was happy to help when people were struggling, and it was a privilege to do so. He was dedicated because he was doing what he loved. After a while, he received special permission from the police chief to take a second job building sheds, and then fishing. He worked harder so we could have a holiday. This, too, was a marker of success. An annual family holiday. This was the time we got to live—to enjoy life to the full, break a few rules, and have the freedom to explore. For a few short weeks, money was not a worry for my family. My father's answer was always, "We work hard. We are on holiday." It was difficult to come back to school and work from this place of holiday feelings—it was as if life was supposed to be hard with periods of relief reserved for holiday times.

Aged twelve, my friends and I were choosing our subjects to study at secondary school. At this time, many of us also had parents going through separation. I was waiting for it to happen to us too. I felt detached from the lessons at school. The pressure of choosing subjects for secondary school seemed trivial compared to the real-world issues my friends and I faced.

By thirteen, I had a paper round, delivering newspapers seven days a week. School felt distant and irrelevant compared to the immediate challenges for my friends and I at home. Did the teachers think they were providing a consistent space, I wonder? For me, school felt very detached from bigger issues. Everything was costing more, but it simply increased my teachers' argument that without school I would not be able to afford anything. I felt the use of fear as a motivator in my school setting. I did not want to ask my parents for more money when it was clear it was already tight and they couldn't work any harder! So I found a way to earn my own pocket money, getting up early each morning, and I shared the money with my younger sister.

A few years later, during a hard-won family holiday to Italy, a pivotal moment occurred. After a heated argument with my mum, a random woman we met on that trip told me that my mother could be my best friend if I let her. This struck a chord. I didn't know why I was angry with my mum at the time. Mum didn't know either, so we clashed. Later during that same holiday, I took a trip to Florence with my mum, where we admired the frescoes and the statue of David. Spending some time together doing what we both loved helped mend our rift at this time.

As I grew older, the pressure to define my future intensified. Although I dreamed of being a writer, the concerns about financial stability loomed large.

I was doing well at school and did not think university was out of the question, until I woke one morning, age seventeen, with an undiagnosed pilonidal sinus at the base of my spine that prevented me from feeling my legs.

Without any warning, I was in hospital undergoing emergency surgery and looking at a lengthy recovery in the midst of my A-levels. My school would not support me in taking the exams with such an extended period of absence, which left me feeling deeply let down. My parents could see the effort I was making to keep up, and paid for my exam entry, but my grades were a long way from those that had been projected. University was a firm No. My grades did not reflect my work, and I remember feeling rather bitter that my schooling and plans had been wasted. My teachers had demanded a focus from me to attain good grades but, through no fault of my own, these could not be achieved without additional support. It was not forthcoming so my dreams and all work up to that date disappeared—like vapour. They vanished. There was no evidence to be passed along for all I had done.

I took a year out and worked in an RAF (Royal Air Force) convalescent home. It was surprisingly healing to meet those who had served in the prime of their life, and hear about their adventures and hardships. This experience helped me get over my own sense of loss and find a new drive.

Seeking a stable career and a home of my own, at nineteen years of age I entered the police service. The ongoing training and professional development in the police service were a revelation, contrasting sharply with the static education system of my school years. I went on to serve twenty years as an officer in England and ended my service in the Channel Island of Guernsey. I've been a tutor, trainer, patrol officer, training supervisor, intelligence officer and, lastly, a fraud investigator. After twenty years of policing, these roles gave me skills I transferred into the Tax Office: Financial Investigations. It was my first effort to strike a better work/life balance for my own family as police life did not value family life.

Reflecting on my early life, I see how the societal pressures of my childhood shaped my adult choices. The emphasis on securing a good job, buying a house, and conforming to societal expectations often overshadowed personal passions and dreams. My reasons for marrying and having children were, in part, due to those expectations—and it takes a strong person to ignore expectations. I even turned to a book when I was about to become a mother, rather than trusting my own intuition. Pregnancy is scripted, birth is scripted, raising a child is scripted. Education is scripted. As are many other aspects of our modern life.

Through policing, I understood the importance of continuous learning and adapting to change. My parents' sacrifices and struggles taught me resilience but, as time has passed, I now see that it's reasonable—if not imperative—to question the systems we live in and pursue a life that balances security with personal fulfilment.

In the end, it's not just about "fitting in" or following a script; it's about finding magic in the unique paths we carve for ourselves, even if they defy conventional expectations. This is the story of how I learned that the magic of not fitting in often leads to the most fulfilling journeys and clearly shows where our current Education, Health, and Justice systems miss the mark.

Yves: Yves is my best friend and husband. We met when I transferred to Guernsey when I was thirty-three, where Yves was a police motorcyclist and traffic officer. At that time I transferred, I was married with a two-year-old son and we were friendly, if not immediate friends.

I was trying to save my marriage when we met. My relationship with my husband was at an all time low of name calling and unpleasantness, despite our move to Guernsey. Home was not a nice place to be. I was totally smitten with my son, however, and desperate to create peace. I made too many allowances for the behaviour of my husband through not wanting to admit I had failed at this relationship thing again.

I had always found relationships difficult.
The pressure to find a boyfriend at school.
The pressure to define myself.
The pressure to marry at a certain age.

At twenty-two as a young police officer, I had mistaken friendship and genuine kindred feelings for another person, and it was a painful experience for both of us. During our relationship, we felt the expectation of marriage, and I felt powerless to explain why I did not feel that way. We were married despite our misgivings, and on our honeymoon—of all places—agreed we had made a mistake. When we returned from that time away, we quickly annulled the marriage. It was a tough time and I didn't really understand why I felt the pressure to marry. He was a wonderful man, whom I cared about deeply, but I was not thinking further than friendship.

This relationship was different. At twenty-nine, when I met the man who was to become my second husband, I was certain that I had found my life partner, despite my family's misgivings. This time I needed it to be right. And it wasn't. Eight years later, I really did not want to accept that it was unsalvageable, but when I found myself praying I could come home and it would just be polite, it made me stop and think that I was setting the bar pretty low for a loving relationship.

When I found the courage to leave my marriage, I was ready to swear off the whole idea of relationships as a painful and exhausting experience.

Enter Yves. With sticky toffee pudding.

A tentative start to the idea of having a relationship again, especially with a young son to care for and unhappy divorce proceedings, nonetheless it was a chance I took—and we have never looked back. He became my very best friend. Finally, I have the "partner" I was seeking, who was also seeking me.

We laugh way more than we cry and, together, we found our way through the quagmire of the legal system, his parents' opinions on our relationship, and that whole stigma about marriage being *hard work* rather than *fun work*.

I realise now that sometimes you have to be brave and challenge yourself to be you and nothing less.

We chose to have another child to complete our little family.

Shock of shocks, we chose to be pregnant before we chose to marry.

George: George is my first son. He birthed me as a mother, a new role I honestly wonder if any of us are truly prepared for. He introduced me to the juggling act that is parenting and working, a completely new approach to food preparation, and the idea that I was responsible—in so many ways—for another person. No wonder I panicked in pregnancy; with hormones raging, I wondered how on earth I would meet all my child's health demands, my child's needs, and return to work in six months with a child who was content, eating and sleeping well, and in a nice routine. So many boxes needed to be checked for this to work, it seemed.

I hit the books, which is what I had learned to do when facing something new. There were times George did not fit the routine defined in the book, and I watched my own mother marvel at my lack of intuition. I was scared to get it wrong; it felt like all eyes were on me to get it right, to do everything the book said, or what the experts knew to be true. In hindsight, it concerns me that there was something considered "right" here. Funny that I relied heavily on my intuition and ability to assess situations at work, but did not feel I could do that with my first son. Was this part of my belief that I had an innate lack of ability when it came to relationships? Regardless, I knew that I didn't want to mess it up with my child.

I adored his black eyes from the first time I saw him, on waking from a caesarean delivery after "failing" to follow the planned script for an easy birth. Instead, I experienced intervention for a more difficult birth. His eyes are grey/blue now and he shares my colouring, on the fairer side. So much love flowed to this little boy, but it was marred with a fear of getting it wrong.

Through his time with a childminder, at nursery, and into junior school, he amazed me with his quick memory, resilience, and natural charm. He was popular and friendly, and knew how to "fit." He could match his behaviour with the expectations made of him in school, rarely skipped a step, and was one of those "upbeat" children. Teachers wanted ten of him in their class. He ate well, slept well, and rarely put a foot out of place.

His father and I were struggling though. Instead of being supported, I felt constant pressure that I was not enough. The home was not clean enough; I was late home from work; the food I prepared was barely edible; I was fast becoming unattractive to him. He couldn't see I was struggling and feeling rather alone in our relationship. All the while I was working to match his salary to be "enough," then handing it over because that was how we had agreed to manage our finances. It began to make me question this balance. But it did not improve, and I felt judged and sneered at for trying, with most of our communication being around how I wasn't what he wanted.

In an effort to meet his needs and balance my love of being a mum, I took George and his half-sister to Disneyland during their 2006 summer holidays, whilst their father went to learn to sail. We travelled with my parents and sister, and I expressed to my sister how nice it would be to go with them and have some help from Mum and Dad. In response, my sister observed that she never expected assistance from our parents and felt I shouldn't be going on a family holiday to receive help. Perhaps she learned, the same as I had, that there was shame in asking for help? My father never asked for help, either.

During the divorce, which was hard on all of us, George's father disappeared about as far away from the UK as he could—to Trinidad and Tobago—giving little information about his plans. He did insist on George being privately educated though; I think he was hopeful that I would see that divorce was not something I could afford, nor was raising a child alone. Did he place obstacles to try and show me how much harder it would be? Would I change my decision, "do the right thing," and stay?

Instead, the court insisted that George's father finance his educational expectations. I was very grateful. George took full advantage of all this school had to offer and quickly found a love of sports. He ran, and played football, rugby, and table tennis. After playing tennis for a while, he decided he was happy to play and join in, but did not really feel the whole "sport thing." His love had morphed into music and singing. These loves filled every waking moment outside of school, and through this, he formed a firm friendship group. There were comments made and fears shared about how this could financially support him going forward and I flashed back to my own parents' concerns about my love of writing; in direct contrast, I chose to support him in shooting for his dreams.

When George entered secondary school, his participation in the school play instilled a further love of acting and performing on stage. As I write, he is finishing his degree in Musical Theatre. At twenty-one, he is entering the workplace and I realise that all he has ever really needed me for is to support and love him through his own journey of self-discovery. During his time at high school, his teachers were his, and my, friends—I thought this experience was more common than not.

George has a rounded intelligence and a passion for all things musical theatre; watching him live his dream is a huge gift. He has an incredible sense of humour and a strong sense of justice. Simply being in his company is a joy to me.

William: When William was born, he stole hearts. Dark-haired and with his father's colouring, those black eyes got me again. I didn't believe it was again possible to love so much. William increased the love I already had for my family, and this love went so much further.

As a baby, he had a way of charming people, calling them to him until he discovered movement for himself and a whole new area opened up. He did not sit still. Ever.

It was not long before my husband and I could clearly see he was not here to "fit." He resisted everything. We tried to have fun with it.

William was just three-years-old when he outgrew the confines of a classroom and created headaches and trauma in a system of "fitting" that belied his years.

A mini-pandemic for our family enshrined in a three-year-old, such was the chaos. He was born in 2011, way before the COVID-19 pandemic, but the lessons he brought for us were equally as impactive.

PART II. EARLY CHALLENGES

WILLIAM'S EARLY YEARS

THIS DIAGNOSIS OF "not fitting in" began in nursery school and triggered a strong reaction in me, partly due to flashbacks of the lack of support I received as a child. I was shocked at how quickly he was turned away. When William was eighteen-months-old, his nursery called to complain that he wouldn't sit and colour like the other children. Instead, he constantly ran outside to play on the tricycles visible through the large windows.

He was always in motion.

Rather than endure daily reports about the challenges the staff faced with our little tornado, we reviewed his situation. William was six months younger than the others in his group and we recognised he might need a different approach. The nursery staff seemed relieved, and the owner was wonderful in acknowledging our perspective. We decided to switch to a childminder—an absolute gem—who understood that William needed activity and a few clear rules. However, he didn't easily follow rules.

At this time, I was conflicted about these "rules." I fully understood that, for his safety and respect for the childminder's furniture, William shouldn't be bouncing all over her sofas. But why did he need a rule about "not chewing the pram handle?" Should we need to explain this to him? As Charlie Brown would say, I had many "Good Grief!" moments.[1]

---

1. Charlie Brown® and Peanuts® are registered trademarks of Peanuts Worldwide LLC.

In an effort to prepare William for school, he started at another nursery school with the full support of his childminder. She was an incredible support to us.

Within a few short months, however, the senior staff at the nursery decided he would not be recommended for their infant school because he was "too disruptive." His older brother had attended this school and, whilst William was "'foetus in utero," I'd been asked by the headmistress to register William to ensure he had a space at their school. Given this, we were stunned to learn so early, especially given his young age, that he was being examined and excluded.

On one particularly memorable day, the staff even advised that he should be checked for "abnormalities," namely autism. He had eaten a LEGO® brick that day, and they wanted him taken to hospital for a scan to ensure that a LEGO city was not lying in his stomach. It was the first time I had heard the word autism associated with William. I rapidly started to put together the little I knew about it, and realised I would have to hit the books again. I knew so very little about autism, but how could I have missed this? Surely not? He spoke pretty well, gave eye contact, didn't "line things up" much, or seem to need a particular order to his day, toys, or routine that I thought to check for. And he ate most of the food I put in front of him. But the nursery teacher felt his speech was unclear. She explained that he made eye contact, but not in a room full of other children and, for his age, was pretty independent and forceful about doing things his way. He had absolutely no thought for his safety, stepping off the very high play equipment whenever he felt like it, and running off whenever the mood seemed to take him.

The hospital visit that followed was another highly judgemental environment. As parents, we come to expect a feeling of being interrogated about why children visit any hospital or medical appointment. I understand the reasoning for it, and behind it, however due to systemic fears of missing the signs of intentional child harm, our Health systems now behave in a way that makes regular parents—whose children experience ordinary accidents—uncomfortable, and those who deliberately harm their children simply avoid the services. This is clearly shown by the dialogue on that day:

Me: "He was at preschool when he swallowed the LEGO brick."

Cue judgemental frown.

Receptionist: "Exactly, how did it happen?"

Me: "I'm sorry, I don't know?"

Nurse: "Exactly, how long has the brick been in there?"

Me: "I'm sorry, they didn't say. They called me at work and told me to bring him straight here. They are not sure how many bricks may be in there and they felt an x-ray would be prudent and should be done immediately."

Nurse: "Did they now? He will probably pass the bricks quite naturally; I'm assuming it was the small LEGO and not childproof bigger bricks?"

Me: "I thought so too, but I guess the concern of the staff is not being sure how many bricks he managed to get in."

Nurse: "I'll get the doctor."

Doctor (following the x-ray): "We can't see any bricks, anything there will pass through naturally, but let's talk about how your child's diet is clearly suffering and why he is putting things in his mouth at his age."

Me: "He eats well."

Doctor: "Yes, he's a big lad, but there will be nutritional deficiencies in what you are providing for him, as children who eat non-food items at his age are not getting the nutrients they need."

Me: "We eat whole foods as a family. I make a lot of it and he eats what we eat."

Doctor: "That's unlikely to be the case, but only a blood test will tell us."

Me: "OK."

Doctor: "It won't be nice for him and I'm reluctant to take blood from such a young one to verify what I know." (*Was he back peddling?*)

Me: "If he has a deficiency that is causing the issue of eating non-food things, then I think I should probably know what that is so I can correct it. Don't you? That is what you need me to do?"

The blood tests came back normal.

Doctor: "I will refer you to the health services so they can start the process of testing for other conditions that may be present."

Being off the hook for not feeding him properly was one thing, I suppose.

Back to school and having been assured that a LEGO city was, in fact, not being quietly built in his stomach, we endeavoured to engage with the pre-school staff only to find that suspected autism firmly closed the doors.

Teacher: "We cannot recommend him for onward placement. He is not a good fit for our school. He does not meet the criteria we have for the children admitted."

Me: "I'm sorry to say this but I believe you are telling me that you are not equipped to service his needs should he be diagnosed with autism?"

Teacher: "We are not really allowed to say. I cannot suggest he is autistic, but given what you have said and the behaviours we have seen, we are very concerned—and no, we don't have to cater for it as a private school. The state (government run) schools have to provide an autism service."

Doors were already closing to William. But I was not at any stage of thinking what might be opening for him.

Rejection and Struggles

Then came the tests and assessments, multiple questions, and investigations. As parents, we were dragged through the mud. I was asked everything from what I ate before pregnancy, what I ate during pregnancy, what I did during pregnancy, even why I needed a medical intervention when William was born (many mums will be familiar with the need for a small episiotomy). I was asked in a way that did not explain that they were collecting data to try and establish the causes of what they suspected to be autism, but in a way that suggested I had, in some way, deliberately acted to cause issues for my child. This exercise was incredibly soul destroying, especially when I was just a mum concerned that my little whirlwind was not "fitting in."

My stress frequently came out in tears.

Having our choices and child micro-analysed caused us to think about what he would need to "fit" into our community. Part of that community was our extended families, and we needed to consider how we included them in these discoveries. Yves and I needed our parents to understand that William would need more support, that he *genuinely* could not "sit and play," and wasn't being "naughty" and requiring discipline or punishment. Consequences would be a lesson for later—when he had the capacity to understand and receive it. Autism was a new education for everyone in William's immediate family, and every single ripple he made beyond us.

Everything William did was different to our recognised methods of measuring child behaviour and development. He came with a force that was hard to encourage to "fit." He was not interested in "fitting." It was, frankly, a little scary for everyone to see this powerful call for change in someone so young.

These events at nursery and beyond led to input that I'm certain that some of our family members felt was helpful, but their words mirrored the scathing views of the community—that ADHD and autism diagnoses were being handed out "all too often" as an "excuse for poor parenting." These words, actually used in media headlines at the time, were considered to be true by some of our family members.[2]

We were faced with extremes of view from our parents about what our young child needed—everything from our choice of the milk he drank due to a lactose intolerance, to discipline and a "good smack," to being forced to "sit until he ate it, or go hungry." Extended families try to help "fix" behaviours, with approaches that they believed worked for them, without ever having been encouraged to look at the causes of the behaviour—we accept a baby cries for food, to be changed, or is tired, but we do not extend this understanding as children age and their behaviours speak to emotions they are struggling with. Our parents believed that by a scripted age, these behaviours should be gone.

We are not the only family to experience this generational change in our approach to parenting. Given that professional advice and intervention have changed so dramatically over the years—let's recall that we used to encourage babies to drink coffee, rub brandy on their gums for teething, and give them bacon and eggs from six weeks of age—is it any wonder that the generations of parents and grandparents following the "advice at the time" come to blows? These differences can divide a family at the very time that a close family is needed for support.

The opinions of William's grandparents were also wildly different from the medical and educational patriarchy oversight we were exposed to at the time, which was to, "watch and observe your child to understand why." We followed medical advice and watched him. We watched his behaviour and asked ourselves what was happening behind it. What was he trying to tell us, or show us, through his behaviour? This approach conflicted with the corrective approach.

It felt as if the health and education services, and our own employer services,

---

2. Paton, Graeme. "Special Needs Used as a Cover for Poor Parenting." *The Telegraph*, May 4, 2012.

were less interested in our observations and more interested in watching us. They watched everything we did and, despite my detective-like, documented, clear, and impartial observations, it was obvious to me that there was only one way with this: "These are the methods that work. You are benefitting from all our knowledge." But this knowledge was learned from a book. And my child was throwing their book out the window. He did not "fit" the profile of "normal," nor did he "fit" the profile of autistic. It was a significant challenge to integrate the observations from education and health workers—and they rarely agreed on the best course forward. Add our parents' views in there, too, and it was a third challenge to meet during our own steep learning curve.

Balancing all this became another hardship to manage when we were already struggling, coming to terms with a diagnosis, and learning what was required to help our child, not to mention what this difference—not fitting the perceived norms—meant for William and our family.

I was caught in a pressure chamber of shame, guilt, and disgrace at home, and again in my work and educational spaces. Gone was the reliable and professional person I knew; gone was the volunteer parent who helped at school activities. She was replaced by the person who rushed out of work, apologising for the lack of notice, needing to be elsewhere to answer a sudden call from the school about her child. She was organised the night before, only to watch it fall apart at the beginning of the school day with her son refusing all efforts to leave the house on time. She felt like all she knew was useless. She was someone I did not recognise as me.

I felt so much:

Shame that I had probably done something to cause this—although nobody knew what. The Sword of Damocles hangs even when we don't know. I was haunted by the judgemental looks from co-workers who wondered why I was always arriving late, or rushing out the door, and the constant requests for consideration at work that "broke the rules."

Disgrace that I was not "managing" my child—that I needed additional support if I was to keep the show all together: Employer happy, School happy, Family happy. √

Guilt—the parent-shaming of those with an autism diagnosis is real! I never felt reading five books a night was enough for everyone who was watching us, especially his support workers who behaved as if I didn't bother to do anything with him. I felt that bath playtime was never enough because I didn't fully understand that he struggled with transition from bath to bed. I felt deeply that what we were doing to support him was never enough. Add to this the absence that my caring for William's needs caused to my husband and eldest son and, well, you get the idea. I felt an overwhelming guilt of not being enough—for anyone. Eventually that spilled out.

> *I recall being in a shop, trying to pick up some family essentials, with our son who was about three-years-old. He was big for his age but was still on child reins to try and keep him safe with me. He absolutely lost any sense, breaking into a wild frenzy in the store and starting to pull things off the shelves.*
>
> *I could have scooped him up and abandoned the project. Later, I did exactly that when faced with this behaviour. At the time I did not understand a key aspect of the situation—that for whatever reason, he had reached saturation point. At that time, though, I desperately tried to place stuff back on the shelf, embarrassed by his outburst. A woman stood over me, tutting, and the man with her announced loudly that there was "another child who needed a damn good smack."*
>
> *My face was hot with embarrassment and humility. I wanted to scream at the man, and at my child, to stop it. I held Will's reins uncomfortably tight as he writhed and fought to escape, and I said nothing—just retching at the lack of anything practical, helpful, useful, supportive, or encouraging. The judgments for my son, and us as his parents, were so keenly felt, everywhere, that I could have sincerely vomited them up.*

A medical diagnosis of autism followed all the explorations, assessments, tests, and home visits. The medical professionals also identified some sensory processing differences that would be challenging to manage. He was seeking noise with one side of his body and calm with the other. No wonder he was confused. He didn't feel pain or consider risk. He couldn't stand the hand dryer in a public bathroom or the sound of other babies crying, and he ran from the noise, unable to communicate what was happening in his body when this experience hit him.

We received the diagnosis about six months after the Accident and Emergency LEGO-eating saga. That's a long time for a parent and child to be so critically under the microscope! We also knew we were fortunate in comparison to other families in Guernsey who were waiting for years!

Shortly after William's diagnosis, the autism specialist in charge of the assessment and diagnosis of the condition left the island. This meant parents were left waiting many more years for a qualified replacement and assessment following their referral. Referrals highlighting concerning behaviours can come from a GP, or from teachers in school. I cannot imagine being left in limbo, dealing with the school complaints, and trying to balance it all for that long; my heart goes out to those families who have no choice but to continue to wait. It also goes out to the teachers who try to work within ridiculous parameters. Teachers who are unable to tell parents their concerns with any clarity, due to feeling they cannot engage with parents about the welfare of their children. Teachers waiting significant periods of time for assessments to give some clarity regarding the care needs of the child. How frustrating must it be for them to finally have the information in hand only to then be told they cannot afford to provide the necessary care, but will have to work with these needs as best they can?

I knew some families who paid a significant amount of money to be privately assessed, only to be advised by the local authority that the diagnostic criteria used by the authorities was different to the one used in assessments.

A local charity explained the different criteria to me, but it still boiled down to a child being unsupported. Without the support of charities such as the National Autistic Society (Guernsey) branch and Autism Guernsey, we would have been completely isolated.[3] They provided us with courses, wider reading, understanding, and support—all without judgement. I will be forever grateful. They were our safe space.

Note that it is charity organisations—not government—who, again, provide support where it is most required. Volunteers. People who are often unpaid, but can see the holes and know where support is desperately needed.

After diagnosis, I didn't feel any of the relief or vindication that I thought I would feel. It felt like such a huge goal to get to the end of the process, and on recognising that we were right about Will, it didn't surprise me that our son needed something different. He could not sit still, so how could he be in a classroom that required this behaviour? He didn't like the scratchy feedback of a pencil on paper—so how would he learn to write? It was going to take a different approach to his education to provide him with the tools for being part of a traditional school community. My only relief was that the six-month assessment process had concluded which meant that William would have support in school so he would no longer be considered "naughty." He would be with people who understood autism: that's what I thought the diagnosis would provide. It's what every parent of an autistic child I have spoken with, or heard from—which number in the hundreds—believes the diagnosis will achieve. More understanding. Less judgement. More skills deployed by support workers who are experienced at working around the challenges our children face with the expected activities and behaviours in school, such as sitting still and using a pencil.

---

3. Learn more about autism, and keep up-to-date with the charity's latest news for Guernsey at autismguernsey.org.gg

But I still felt wronged by the process. I felt angry. I felt overwhelmed by what this may mean for my child. In a world where day-to-day life was hard enough, why did he deserve this extra challenge? Why, for that matter, did we?

I spent a good few months going over and over the questions they had asked me, wondering what on earth I did before, during, and after pregnancy that could have caused this. Each day he struggled, I was left wondering what role I had played. The whole process left me feeling as if I was to blame, and I found it close to impossible to break the cycle of wondering what I had done to cause these extra challenges for him. Guilt became my way of being, and I honestly felt I needed to apologise for everything: to my family, George, William, his teachers, and my workplace.

Fortunately, I confessed my confusion and concerns to a visiting nurse who worked alongside the special educational needs group that was looking at how to support our son in school. She covered my hand with her own and said, "They don't know the causes of autism and that's why they asked you everything like that. It was not intended to make you feel like you did something wrong."

In hindsight, I imagine what could have happened had I not been so open with her, and how much harder I would have been on myself but for the want of this simple explanation. My thoughts had kept me up at night, as I agonised over what I ate and how this happened. I fixated on the many questions asked about my diet, the cat who had fleas, and why I'd fumigated the house when I was pregnant. I had checked that it was OK, but was it really? I wonder how many mothers don't have this explanation and are left worrying after the diagnostic process that leaves us feeling blameworthy. It was purely chance that it was explained to me.

This wasn't the first time I had considered the unintended harms our systems bring, and the countless ways hurried and overworked essential workers cause unintended harms. As a serving police officer, I had also experienced this, mostly as a result of poor communication and consideration. Harms that were never intended but, with a bit of time and care, could have been prevented. There are greater harms, too, that come from not developing the community in line with the evidence in hand, but that's another story entirely.

The Educational Determination followed his diagnosis—a golden plan that explained the high levels of additional support our son would need to attend school, and outlined the special provisions that would be made to support him.

I felt like I had won the lottery and this reinforced my belief that he would receive support, understanding, and guidance in line with knowledge of why he behaved the way he did. Other families struggle on without a plan that provides clear direction for staff to refer to. Some teaching staff see the need and simply fill it without having such a plan in place, as they know the backlog of children waiting for assessments is just woeful.

Gold plan in hand, I felt relief that our son would not be judged for his behaviour. In fact, he would be understood. He would be with people who worked with children like him, would not be forced to accommodate what he could not be expected to, and he would be supported in this drive to get him to "fit" with what was required. The diagnostic process may have been ongoing and a little traumatic, but it was worth it because all the people around him now understood he was not "naughty." He had autism and some sensory processing differences that we would come to better understand, over time.

Groups of people would be required to work hard with our youngest towards that "fit." For the first time in over a year, we felt less alone, less ostracised, and less judged. There was no question though: He must be made to "fit."

I didn't question it either.

Not then.

I understood it all from a systemic point of view, but did not have enough information to begin to understand what this school environment would be like for him.

Starting the School Process

William began to attend a "special" nursery. We stopped receiving the daily complaints and, instead, heard reports on what he *could* do. What a difference that made! Honestly, I felt like I was flying. We had done it. In Guernsey, Channel Islands, UK, where the slow and delayed diagnostic process was the source of constant complaints, and a huge queue waited, we had managed to get through. It was a shallow victory in light of the larger picture, but I was trying to stay afloat. Sometimes you have to come away from the bigger picture and survive the little one so you can have the energy to impact it later.

William's support worker at the nursery expressed her concerns that he was nowhere near ready to start school. She offered no blame here. She simply observed what we all saw. I agreed with her. She had spoken with the placement team, however, and they were not of a mind to extend his time within the nursery. She was concerned that his placement was short term and considered he may benefit from a longer-term placement.

I enquired into deferring his school start date and was offered all manner of reassurance that he would be "fine" to start school at the specified time. The man controlling this would become the most shapeshifting individual and, to this day, I cannot decide if he intentionally misled us, or if he had some other unspoken need led by the State's body for Education.

His department had support workers in place who were looking forward to meeting William. There were so many platitudes: "I think he's rather wonderful," "He's certainly a character, but we are used to this and he'll be just fine." I explained (and hoped to goodness I was not getting a good nursery teacher into any trouble), that we and his current support felt he was not ready. As he was born in June, he was only a couple of months off the cut-off date in August where a parent could choose to defer starting school for a year.

This man's response was to say that if William did not start on time, the support he had been offered would be swiftly removed and we could not expect it in a deferred year.

This is similar to denying access to funding for tertiary students who take a "gap year" because they believe their personal development lies outside the fields of academia for a while. Yves fell victim to this policy when he left school at sixteen and, like so many young people, was not sure of the path he wanted to take. He did know he needed a break from all the study. After almost a year out of school, his love of sports and fitness had him consider working in physiotherapy, but to study would mean he could not receive any financial support for the off-island education, purely because he had taken a "gap year." If he had stayed on at school, he would have received this financial support, as the island offers no higher education facilities and all students beyond A-level head off-island to continue their studies. Yves was faced with the decision as a teenager to take the break he knew he needed, or lose any hope of funding. The system in place even then did not consider the need or wellbeing of the learner.

But with William, the threat of having our new-found support removed was too much.

"There are forty other children here who need support who won't get it. If he doesn't take this space now, as the privilege offered to him, with all we have put in place for him, he won't get it in the future."

Such pressure, with an equal measure of sadness. Forty children not receiving support? Are parents really being forced to compete for support?

One parent explained to me how grateful she was for her teaching and education background, as without it she was confident her child would not have been identified as in need of support. After our discussions, we agreed there is a specific language around the culture of education which, if you are less than fluent in it, means you will not tick the required "buzz words" or boxes.

Not knowing the right language to use will, at best, mean a delay as you continue to push and push to be understood about why your child needs support. At worst, it means the child is never recognised, and goes through school wondering why they struggled with things that neurotypical people do not. Often, children conclude there is something wrong with them, which may end up with rebellion, or even withdrawal into themselves in ways that are potentially harmful. Many parents who are supporting neurodivergent children believe that they must consistently advocate for their child, and often fight an uphill battle for recognition of their child's needs against a system that requires conformity to work. Catering for "difference" incurs higher costs, after all.

As a result of the threat to remove support before it had even started, William began school "on time." But not in *his* time. Not at the time that would be most beneficial to *him*. It had to be when the system said so. In a queue, with all the other little uniforms, bag in hand, and excitement on his face, his journey began. I hoped it would be as positive as I had been assured.

In the first few weeks, William showed them his "force of Will," his running away, and his inability to sit still. I collected him to the tune of, "Not a good day Mrs. Lenormand," from his support worker.

He ran through puddles and was corrected. He refused to play with children wearing red shoes.

> *One morning in the playground, he struck me in front of his teacher because he could not wait to line up. His teacher shouted at him in front of me, "Mr. (name withheld) would never hit his mummy." But the staff could see I was being hit and didn't record it or intervene any further. I felt like they simply handed him out to me and ignored what they could see. There was no invitation to discuss this behaviour towards me or others, just a blanket assessment that it was not acceptable to hit children in school, as if I was unaware of that. He was hitting out at many people, which was his way of communicating distress—and that was being ignored.*

They also didn't ask questions when I explained how aggressive he was at home. This aggression was increasing with his lack of understanding and frustration. When I spoke up and asked for help, the teachers, support workers, and educational psychologists nodded. Just nodded.

I began to wonder why I was sharing information with them at all. I thought we were working together to support William? I needed to understand why he was hitting, and how we could stop him.

He used the latch on the gate to escape from the playground, something they did not anticipate, despite me voicing my concern that he would do just that. He had certainly become quite the Houdini in escaping from the house to the coveted outside.

> *"Not a good day again today, Mrs. Lenormand." People stared as this was declared by his support worker, who was struggling down the stairs on crutches with a smile on her face. But it was not a friendly smile, it was a passive acceptance that all was not well and there was nothing she could do about it. I began to intensely dislike pick-up time with its daily complaints, these little announcements in front of everyone. This was not what I had envisaged when they said he would receive "support." This support was a daily level of critique that was exhausting and left me numb with disappointment. I found myself explaining to parents that William had autism, in an effort to help them understand why he was not achieving what their child was in the way of manners and super self-control. Some were kind, and we talked. Others shrugged it off as meaning he should not be near their children. As his parents, Yves and I experienced both sides of this fence.*

William was sent off to speech therapy in that first year because the teacher could not understand his words. The speech therapist could not see the issue so, after one assessment session, the speech therapist and I agreed that he spoke rather nicely and was easy enough to understand. Then we had Occupational Therapy sessions. Yes, he liked to move—a lot. Spinning around stimulated his system and he sought this, but he also sought swinging "back and forth" to calm himself. He appeared to be trying to self-regulate and needed space to do that. None of these sensory movements were helped by sitting in chairs in a classroom. He could leave for movement breaks *if* someone was available and *if* the space was available. Again, not the support we had been advised would be there for him.

Support staff were changing, being moved, and they had their own illness and staffing issues. This all meant that the support promised was not delivered. But anyone who has worked in government service knows the battle between needing staff, and training and budget constraints. These teachers and support staff were not getting what they wanted, and needed, to support our children in any way.

At this time, I concluded that this "fit" they were aiming to achieve was a minimum standard that was absolutely required to be learned by William as a three-year-old child with autism, simply because he had so much school life in front of him.

There are differing responses, too, depending on the age of the child at the time they receive their diagnosis. William was three, going on four. Some support workers believe that a diagnosis of a child so young could be incorrect. The response to those diagnosed later, such as the case of my friend with twins—one diagnosed and one still fighting for it—is different again. The attitude towards families whose autism diagnosis has come later—after years of concern in a number of cases—was not to worry about the "fit" at that stage. By secondary school, these twins were "left to fend for themselves." They have managed thus far. Families such as my friend's fight to have the symptoms they experience in the "safe" place of the home even recognised. Many report that school notes indicate they see "no such trouble at school," even though the child's behaviour at home—where they feel safe to express themselves—shows a very different story.

Some children, as we experienced with William, can learn to "mask" their behaviours and needs until they get home. As he aged, we stopped seeing so much of his evident hardships in the classroom and, instead, experienced them at home, where he was safe and free to explode all the things he had contained for the day. This makes home life extremely challenging and hard on families. The further downside is the school staff don't see what the child is actually going through and insinuate to parents that it's not happening at school so it must only be at home. There is an evident lack of understanding that the safe place of home is where some neurodivergent children explode the entirety of the feelings, thoughts, and natural behaviours they have suppressed for the day. They hide it in the understanding that the wholeness of them and the way they learn is "not allowed in school." Unable to communicate their anxiety and fears at the time, they come out at home, and are then refuted by teachers. Other children "go into themselves," wondering what on earth is wrong with them, and isolate themselves at every opportunity to protect themselves from the people, rules, and judgements they do not understand.

There is no "one size fits all" with autism. It does not go away. It presents differently, individually, in each of the people who experience it.

As they mature, and by virtue of age again for the purpose of laws and support services, these children are expected to have understanding of things they have never really understood. In my experience, "understanding" is not the linear thing my son so often seeks.

In fact, in many places throughout the UK, all support services stop when the child turns eighteen years of age. It's as if their needs disappear overnight. Unless the child has managed to achieve a separate diagnosis, they become lost in the systems we use in the world.

Mental illness is accepted as accompanying the autism diagnosis, and the practice is to get in early and hope it doesn't happen, rather than teach the tools aligned with the child to support them in managing their own mental health. If there is no intervention by the time they reach secondary school, the practice reflects that the children are too far gone, or in some cases, "Well, they have managed this far."

The focus is on survival rather than any quality of life.

For so many children diagnosed with this condition and other neurodivergent presentations, the system does its best within highly defined parameters that are just too rigid for the complexity of autism and the accompanying presentations, as varied as they are. The people in this system work their hardest to ensure that these children will be able to provide service to their community through some kind of future employment, but this goal is far too narrow. In trying to fit this goal, many gifted and talented children are having their brilliance missed unless there is an academic measurement that can be applied to it.

And that narrow aim starts very early.

Challenging the Trauma

William's Rainbow

Near the beginning of his "school life," our son told me that he simply did not understand how to "get on the rainbow."

I understood this was a behaviour chart on the wall of his classroom which depicted a way of assessing behaviours in class that day, ranging from a dark cloud of stormy, unacceptable behaviour, to a white cloud of, still cloudy, but manageable behaviour. It then progressed to the "sunshine," which was the aim for students and represented what I understand to be a bright and warm day of good behaviour, where many children found themselves after having followed the classroom rules. They sat still at sitting still time, did their work, and had not complained or been any type of nuisance that day. Lastly there was a coveted "Rainbow"—reserved only for the exceptional child who surpassed this "Sunshine of Wonderfulness."

William wanted to be seen as an exceptional child. He tried so hard to sit still but it hurt him to do so. I spent months trying to help him achieve the coveted "rainbow" placement, which he (aged three/four), did not make in his entire school year. Every day for months, he left the class looking downtrodden, accompanied by his support worker who advised, "It's not been a good day, Mrs. Lenormand." I ended up thoroughly disliking the sight of her cheerful face telling me he had tried his best but, essentially, all his efforts had failed.

> *I had to admire our boy's resilience when he left class one day in that year. Our son encouraged his equally-diagnosed friend to approach me and say that William had made it onto the rainbow. My boy followed, beaming, and I had absolutely no reason to doubt he had achieved his goal. I ruffled his hair, congratulated him on his hard work, and asked how it had happened. He looked confused. Then his friend looked confused.*
>
> *I realised then that they had made it up. Bless them. My son had encouraged his friend to lie, and neither had expected any follow-up questions to aid me in understanding how the success had occurred!*
>
> *Very gently I said, "It doesn't matter to me about the rainbow, you are on my rainbow every day."*
>
> *They looked at me and his friend, having served his purpose, shrugged his shoulders and ran off to his mum. My son, bless him, said, "I just wanted to see what it would feel like. I wanted you to hear I had done it."*

My heart was so full of love for him. So desperate to see what it would "feel like," he had crafted it for himself, just to know. He wanted to see if there was a change in *me* if he achieved his goal. I realised how vitally important it was to give him context to these events in school, that I must assure him that I KNEW he was *genuinely* doing his best to conform. That I, in no way, judged him for not being on the rainbow and he was in no way less to me.

Rethinking the Behaviour Measurement

This event prompted me to consider why our schools feel they must measure behaviour in young children. The concept of measuring children's behaviour in schools raises questions about our educational priorities and the potential harm it may cause to more natural ways of learning and developing. We monitor children daily, tracking their compliance with tasks, goals, and rules, while rewarding or punishing their performance based on set standards. At first glance, this approach—offering rewards like stickers, certificates, and praise for good behaviour, and sanctions for bad behaviour—seems straightforward. Yet, this system may oversimplify the complexities of children's development, focusing more on control and compliance than on meaningful learning.

Why do we feel the need to measure children's behaviour so closely? Part of the answer lies in the desire to manage large groups and ensure uniformity in outcomes. But when this focus on measurement and compliance becomes central to education, as it had with William by becoming his central focus and way of valuing himself, we risk diminishing children's natural curiosity, creativity, and engagement with learning. While some rules, such as those related to safety, are necessary, others—like dress codes or arbitrary conduct rules—seem increasingly disconnected from the core purpose of education. These rules can feel restrictive, making children question their relevance and even hindering their sense of individuality and personal expression.

The reward system also raises concerns. For example, the practice of rewarding children simply for 100% attendance may shift the emphasis away from actual learning and growth. What does it teach children when showing up is valued over their intellectual or emotional development? We've reached a point where merely being present is celebrated, even though attendance alone does not guarantee engagement or success. The emphasis on attendance has also become a political issue, with rising numbers of children refusing to attend school post-pandemic. However, rather than exploring why children are disengaged, the system responds by tightening enforcement of attendance policies—focusing solely on who is present, not on the reasons behind their absence.

Behaviour, when treated as something to be measured and managed, overlooks the fact that children's actions often communicate deeper issues—such as dissatisfaction with the learning environment or struggles with mental health.

Standardised behaviour charts or reports don't account for the wide range of social, emotional, and developmental needs present in any given classroom, particularly for neurodiverse children. For children with autism or other neurodevelopmental differences, traditional behaviour expectations can be especially challenging. Instead of accommodating their unique needs, we isolate them for failing to conform to rigid standards, calling it "inclusion" when, in practice, it often looks like exclusion, when simple considerations are not permitted to deviate from the path.

This brings up a critical issue: Why are there so few alternatives for children who struggle in traditional school environments? The current system lacks flexibility, and families who need specialised or alternative learning environments often face significant financial barriers. This leaves many parents with limited options as public schools are not equipped to offer the variety of learning environments or accommodations some children need to thrive.

In the end, we have to ask: What are we really measuring? By focusing so much on compliance, attendance, and behaviour management, we may be neglecting children's deeper needs for exploration, personal growth, and meaningful learning experiences. I believed his school was missing what William was actually learning from the way he was weighed, measured, and found wanting. What may have started with good intention was not reviewed in light of the evidence before the staff.

School Punishment and Adult Justice Systems

When comparing the systems of punishment and reward in schools to those in the UK adult community, particularly in the areas of misdemeanour and punishment, striking parallels emerge in how both systems prioritise compliance over understanding and rehabilitation. Both institutions rely heavily on punitive measures, where the aim seems to be enforcing conformity rather than fostering growth, empathy, or deeper learning.

In schools, punishments often escalate from mild forms of discipline like shame and embarrassment to more severe actions, such as removing free time or confining movement—mirroring aspects of incarceration in the adult justice system. For instance, students might be placed in isolation or detention, which mimics the isolation experienced in prison, where movement and autonomy are restricted. Both systems remove individuals from the community as a form of punishment, rather than addressing the underlying issues behind their behaviour.

This method of punishment, both in schools and prisons, is often ineffective in addressing root causes. It can generate fear and anxiety but does little to foster true behavioural change. Just as prisons see high rates of recidivism, schools often see repeated misbehaviour, suggesting that punishment alone is not a successful teaching tool. In fact, this approach can create a cycle of stress, fear, and non-compliance, contributing to the rising rates of anxiety in both children and adults.

The Escalating Structure of Control

Schools are environments of increasing structure and discipline, where children are taught to conform to a set of rules and standards from an early age. Play and exploratory learning, which are natural ways for children to understand the world, are undervalued, replaced by rigid preparation for "big school" and standardised assessments.

The purpose of punishment in both systems is often stated as correcting behaviour, yet the evidence shows that punitive measures are far from effective in creating lasting change. In schools, punishments like detention or exclusion don't necessarily teach children why their behaviour was problematic or how to improve. Similarly, in the justice system, prisons are frequently criticised for failing to rehabilitate offenders, instead perpetuating a cycle of crime and punishment.

A more successful alternative is a restorative approach, both in education and justice. I was fortunate to have some training in this area. In schools, restorative practices encourage students to reflect on their actions, understand the harm they may have caused, and work toward making amends within the community. This fosters empathy, accountability, and a sense of belonging, which can help prevent future misbehaviour, simply by hearing and understanding the issues when given space to do so. Similarly, restorative justice in the adult community focuses on dialogue, understanding, and reparation, aiming to heal both the offender and the community rather than simply punishing the individual.

We often miss the opportunities to foster understanding as a powerful tool for change, and create greater traumas in an effort to correct situations quickly.

Conformity vs. Understanding

Both the school system and the justice system appear to prioritise conformity over true understanding. Children who fail to adhere to school rules are often punished rather than given the support they need to understand their behaviour. In the justice system, adults are incarcerated for breaking the law, but little effort is made to understand the personal or social factors that led to the offence, unless it's for those facing severe mental health challenges. In both cases, the focus is on making individuals "fit" into a system, rather than helping them navigate their unique challenges.

This approach fails to recognize that behaviour is often a form of communication. In children, misbehaviour can signal unmet emotional needs, frustration, or difficulty with regulation—whether they are neurodiverse or neurotypical. Similarly, in adults, criminal behaviour may be a response to systemic failures, personal crises, or mental health issues. Isolating individuals—whether in a detention room or a prison cell—does little to address these root causes and often exacerbates feelings of disconnection and alienation. Yet, in both cases, the goal of this punishment—to correct behaviour or prevent future infractions—is often unmet. Instead, isolation can deepen feelings of rejection, anxiety, and hostility.

For adults, we recognize that incarceration should be reserved for those who pose a genuine risk to others, and even then, rehabilitation is key. However, many lesser offences—particularly those related to substance use, minor thefts, or personal struggles—are better addressed through restorative justice rather than imprisonment. Similarly, in schools, children who struggle to regulate their emotions or behaviour may benefit more from understanding and support than from exclusion. The trouble is, the schools need the resources to address these. They need funding and training, and neither is forthcoming.

Shifting from Compliance to Community

The aspect missing is genuine community and embracing diversity in peers. William's school had countless opportunities to change the story here and engage and explain with young minds about the differing needs and considerations for their peers. These opportunities were lost in favour of the tired and scripted punishment and reward system. This approach, however, overlooks the complexity of human behaviour and fails to address the underlying causes of misbehaviour or crime. By adopting restorative practices, schools and justice systems alike can move toward fostering true understanding, community, and personal growth. This shift would better serve both children and adults by creating environments that support rehabilitation, learning, and inclusion, rather than fear and conformity.

Trauma Aware: One Size Does Not Fit All

William's story about being on the rainbow prompted me to discuss with the supporting staff the need to have a daily achievable goal for him, but it was clear that the rainbow was not a negotiable thing and was only rewarded at the end of each day to the most deserving and well-behaved children. They all tried to get on it and exceptions could not be made. *Why?*

We all knew he was going to struggle with all the rules throughout the day.

What about a morning reward? Should we continue to set an unachievable goal? What effect does that have on a child?

"The children know that William is naughty, so they will feel unfairly treated if he gets special consideration."

Ahh, an inflexible system meets an inflexible response. And please don't get me started on the fact that our son had already been written off as "naughty" by his peers and the classroom teachers, despite the golden educational plan in hand.

Teachers did not discourage the shaming towards him because they considered the peer assessment might be the thing to change his behaviour.

I wanted to bloody scream at the evident sheer lack of understanding. *What? Autism changes because of another kid's opinion?* It was either scream or hit my head on a brick wall because the teaching staff did not understand that inducing a sufficient level of *shame* was NOT a cure for the issues we faced.

But that's the current teaching model. Punishment and reward. We encourage children to aim for reward—even if they don't want to do the task—to avoid punishment.

We have something very wrong here.

Once I understood "his" autism and William's need to communicate through his behaviour, I grew past parenting by shame. A simple "Early Bird Course" that teaches parents about autism made it pretty plain. If you are lucky enough to receive this course upon diagnosis, you will learn about a host of needs our children have that are not met by current systems. One of my biggest learning points was to view William's behaviour as an iceberg.

What was happening above the surface, where we could all see it, was often in response to the vast feelings happening underneath the surface that we could not necessarily see. William frequently tried to explain what had happened and found himself unable to understand it well enough to explain it. He became frustrated with his inability to articulate and have another person understand, so he gave up trying. Key parts of learning were being missed and, as parents, we were at a loss to fill in the gaps.

If you read *Changing Our Minds* by Clinical Psychologist Naomi Fisher *(2021)*, you will uncover a wealth of research regarding why we, as a society, prefer to teach in schools the way we do—and it has nothing to do with the best interest of the child or how children learn best. This is quite shocking when you consider all Law to do with working with children starts with "what's in the best interest of the child."

Such a conflict. Quite an eye-opener.

> *By far the worst moment for us as parents was when William was aged six. We had finished his fifth book at our nightly reading time (an agreed limit of five short books a night), when he calmly said that it was all "getting too hard," and he felt it would be better if, "I could just tell him how to die," and wanted to know, "if it would hurt?"*
>
> *I was distraught. I'm not sure if he could see that on my face or not. Sincerely wanting to die at the age of six because it was all too hard and he did not think he should be here?*
>
> *It floored me.*
>
> *In his way, he had worked out that this was the best course of action. To not be here. It felt hopeless to keep trying to fit in.*

We were missing something huge in the way he learns. His loving family was, obviously, not enough to stop this pain. I informed the school support section—and they kindly patted me and made a note of it.

They expect mental health difficulties of autistic children, you see.

It was not even news to them.

I was approaching a breakdown. Not able to sleep through overwhelming fear and worry. Unable to communicate effectively to improve the situation at school for my son was not an experience I was used to. The patronising response to this beggared belief. The unadulterated acceptance that children with autism often have serious mental health issues—and surprise—that I was somehow unaccepting of this. The school records gently reflected, "Mum—not coping well, needs to accept diagnosis if she wants help."

Mum not coping well? What about Mum not writing off her son who had, somehow in this fiasco, concluded there is no place on this earth for him if he doesn't fit the model? Mum is not coping? What about education as a system is not coping with meeting the needs of the neurodiverse community of children it was tasked with supporting? It may be cost effective to state level education—but what about the cost to the child? To the medical system having to unpick the trauma of unmet need? And as for accepting his diagnosis, I was not the one complaining about him every day, calling me at work and asking me to come and get him, or denying him school trips because of his behaviour, which was part of his diagnosis. I wanted to hold up a mirror.

The support staff had become immune to such comments from children in their care, and used to seeing parents distraught to a level it made them ill—the educational support staff were comfortably numb, with the exception of a few. These minor miracles parented children with special needs themselves.

During 2017 at William's school, the children with additional needs were accommodated in a portacabin. These children, who all struggled with social and sensory difficulties, were placed in an echoey shed between three loud playgrounds! Many of the children removed their shoes and tiptoed around it to avoid the noises inside. And, with windows on every wall, the children could see the others playing outside—where they were not permitted to be. Neurodivergent children may not have the social skills to "play nicely" with others, but they sure know what fun looks like, and they feel it when they are not allowed it.

And let's not forget that this was in the wealthy Island of Guernsey in the British Channel Islands. A financial hub and centre of all things offshore—spewing wealth and abundant living with large yachts and private meetings in expensive hotels—yet unable to provide more than a shed for these children.

I'll also share with you that I was told we should be "grateful" for this space. When William started there, it was, in fact, only half the size—but one year later, the original "shed" had become a full portacabin.

Now, I am well aware of how powerful it is to feel genuine gratitude for all we have, but the gall of the staff to suggest we need to be grateful as an excuse not to seek something fit for purpose is not the same.

Over time, I came to realise that they were passing onto me their low expectations about ever receiving appropriate staff, cover, materials, and services. They could no more access the full extent of the resources they needed than I could.

I thought about creating a Freedom of Information request to establish how many meetings they had received to request resources that were denied. I still think that would be a valuable exercise, but haven't done so as it is pointless when nobody wants to listen to, or act on, the information that has been revealed, even though it could be used to inform change in the education system. Others are aware and not able to action it for whatever their reasons are for it not ranking highly enough in the budget constraints.

During this time, our fabulous family doctor noted how ill the whole matter was making us all. My whole body cried out in stress with the sudden onset of Menorrhagia, fainting spells, and the inability to stop crying in frustration. The telephone calls from school into work became so bad that I was nervous each time my work or mobile phone rang, worried I would be required to leave whatever I was doing at work and "come and get him."

Our son was too young for this level of external judgement, one that was rapidly turning into a mountain of internal problems. The pacifying comment that, "Our children often have mental health issues," was no support, comfort, or solution as to why, as a demographic, there is such a rise.

If we know this, we must understand why and stop creating the illusion of inclusion.

"They receive the world differently."

"They cannot filter out the things neurotypicals can."

"He can't sit still."

We use these phrases frequently in our communication about any neurodivergence, without wondering if there is a message from these children that we have something very wrong in the systems that make up our society. The cogs and wheels keep turning in a relentless drive to get to some perceived goal that doesn't come close to one the individual is seeking.

The trauma that accompanied this "not fitting" child was a modern-day horror story. It's taken me over three years to be able to review the memories that are full of blame, persecution, judgement, and fear. These systems we cling to for Education, Health, and Justice lack fundamental human compassion and simple understanding that we are not all here to be the same.

Take Two of These and Be Quiet, Please.

When the school suggested medication for William, I recall the sudden understanding that hit me: an "automaton" was more welcome than my child. The teacher proudly informed me of children who had real success when medicated, because they were quiet and compliant.

In 2016 and 2017, William's support workers were suggesting ADHD medication and, maybe, a referral for an additional diagnosis as the best way to support our child.

In observation of the current criticism levied at Artificial Intelligence, I wonder: Is this not the very outcome our conventional and conforming education system is aiming for? A person who can learn and churn data faster than we can measure, a person who does not push back or seek to be individual, and who exceeds expectations in all tests. Check √

This was a crunch point for me. My child was to be referred to another doctor and possibly medicated to make it easier for the teacher to manage him in a classroom. A classroom he did not understand—and his efforts to communicate this and his distress were to be "medicated."

Not because he needed it, but because the teacher did.

Please understand, I felt for her. Heck, there were days I could have used him having a nap or zoning out too, just so I could get on with everything I needed to do. But can you imagine a parent devising ways to medicate their child to sleep, or into a stupor, because they needed it to be a bit easier? In the realms of law enforcement and the social care of children, you would be staring down the barrel of child abuse claims. But here we were, using prescribed medication as the only answer left in an ineffective educational system.

In my view, medicating our son's behaviour was not going to teach him the expectations of those around him, and was in no way helping him "fit." It was denying him his outlets and enabling the teacher to continue without disruption. Medication was the way to make him "fit" the classroom environment—by denying him access to himself. Is this why we were experiencing his mental health crisis? Was his behaviour not just his way of communicating, "ENOUGH!"?

As a quick fix, it's undeniably easy. But, as a long-term learning tool, I was unconvinced. Our education system is not evolving to manage neurodivergence in schools that accommodate children without recognised "Special Educational Needs." This is a stretched system that is still appalled by, and desperate to resolve, any disruption to its scheduled programme.

If we understand why, we need to address it. We had to insist, firmly, on some support so that we could support our son.

The parents of William's peers could also see why all our children were struggling. These parents became an integral part of our support group, as each of us were subjected to a system that considered itself to be supportive, when the reality was that it was a long way from that. As parents, we discussed that we would have mental health issues if we were forced, as our children were, to feel wrong, different, and out of place. Many of us were struggling for the first time with our own mental health challenges that had developed from trying to survive the pressure of school and work, because our children were not 'fitting." Unable to respond as our children needed us to, because of the poor educational service, was also causing significant mental health strain for all of us. Variations of powerlessness and frustration have beset us all.

It all fell on the deaf ears of a system unable to respond.

For our family, it all came to a head one day in October 2017, as I watched our young son avoid his uniform, then breakfast, and all the things that came with getting ready for school. He looked miserable and was pulled deeply into his feelings. I realised that, for too long, he had been looking miserable and undernourished in all the ways that matter to a young child.

I felt it keenly.

I wanted to cry for him because that was all I had left.

My visit to the GP to share the problems resulted in me bursting into tears and being unable to stop. I was given antidepressants, but they removed the ability to cry even when I needed to.

I was numb, and it was of no help to William for me to be numb. It was not fair, not proportionate, and not reasonable to make him "fit."

Was it even necessary?

Proportion and necessity are keystones enshrined in Human Rights Law, after all. So I went back to what I knew and started to ask the hard questions.

Why was this so difficult? In my mind, the system that had been managing this for years was no more equipped to manage than I was. I needed to consider this again, as it appeared my belief was entirely wrong.

What had they been doing with everyone before us? We had tried so many different ways. So far beyond tired, I was utterly distraught with the lack of compassion in the "education services" that were often anything but supportive or focussed on service-to-my-child.

On that October morning, as we approached the front door, I stopped, looked at Yves, and said, "I'm done. I can't do this to him anymore." Yves agreed, so we stayed home with William and risked the wrath of an imperfect attendance certificate.

Our lack of attendance that day prompted phone calls and denials that things were anything like William, or we, described when we explained why he would not be at school.

They were very comfortable calling him a liar. Then they moved onto us, as his parents.

It had taken me a good while to understand that William saw things differently, valued things differently, and often explored his fears and anxieties through creative stories. The teachers used these "Social Stories" to give him guidance on acceptable behaviours. William explored all avenues of social questioning, without any filter or boundary, by imagining a situation and playing it out verbally as a story, in order to see the response. The response took time for him to process and then question and try out again before he formed a linear understanding of it. A bit like he learned to understand the little world around him with "Getting on the Rainbow." What he struggled to do was to apply his understanding to the situation at hand. That was where he needed extra support and encouragement, and an explanation of why it applied. It caused him no end of frustration that one person liking a game did not mean that another person would like the same game. Linear thinking, or "dealing in absolutes" was his preference—he struggled when it did not apply to everything.

That day was a breakthrough for us as a family. We chose to rally around William, to hold him and show him that we heard him. To recognise he had done his very best here and it was not working, and that this fact did not make him bad or wrong in any way. It meant something needed to change for him and, right then, we didn't know what that something was, but we wanted him to know we would stand with him to find out what it was.

When the school denied his experiences of being "wrong" all the time, not understanding how to please his teacher, and objected to our reasons for keeping him home for the day, we understood that it was going to take more than a day away from school for William to have any kind of recovery. We advised the school that the support he was receiving was not, in fact, supporting him and that we needed to reconsider what we were doing.

Once it was clear we were not moving on his "wellbeing," a new educational psychologist came to our home to work out how we could move forward to help William.

This educational psychologist had just moved to Guernsey from the UK. The meeting went well, and it was clear she understood why we had decided to withdraw him from school. She encouraged us to attend a meeting with the support staff and their supervisor, the Head of Autism and Communication Support at "The Base," to see what we could work out. This was the man who had placed him there and encouraged us to make William start on time, while consistently assuring us all would be well.

There were horrified looks when, in yet another development meeting, we announced our thoughts and considerations to the school. I explained the transition I could see in William was worrying us. I had gone from being hit with lunchboxes the minute we got into the car at school pick-up, followed by evenings of distress and anger from him, through to our child constantly saying he did not understand. I was powerless to explain to William what was happening in school because the support staff were at pains to report his behaviour, *but not what happened surrounding it* so I could help him.

I referenced an earlier meeting when William, aged five, had moved from Reception and into the first year and the support worker wanted to place him on the "Violent Child Register" to enable the team to restrain him. They had some training in restraint techniques but knew nothing of how to watch for positional asphyxia, so I refused. A heavy person in the wrong position on a child can easily cause more distress and hinder their ability to breathe. Most police officers are trained to be aware of this during restraint but the school staff wanted to use restraint without this awareness.

They were insistent that I give my support, which I offered in the form of my attendance at the school, but that was not what they desired. The support staff were upset that I would not support the restraint, despite my explaining why.

What had happened to suddenly require him to be considered a violent child? The support staff explained that on that day, our son had thrown a shoe at a teacher who was trying to get him out from under the desk.

During the meeting about this, I went back over the story numerous times in an attempt to establish how he had ended up under the desk. It was not clear what the trigger was to the support staff member with him; according to her, he simply became upset and hid under the desk and would not come out. I asked why he could not be left to come out of his own accord, and she explained that trying to get him out was disturbing the other children in the class. The teacher wanted him out from under the desk and, as he wouldn't come out, they tried to grab him—and that's when he took off his shoe and threw it at her.

During this conversation, it became clear to me that our child had become distressed about something—distressed enough to hide—and the situation was not managed well. What would have been the harm in sitting near him, waiting for him to calm and come out of his own accord, and then discussing it? Why couldn't the teacher have encouraged the other children to simply continue and ignore it, please?

I could see William was struggling to give the behaviour they wanted, and now, with my "big girl pants" firmly on, I drew a line under all our earlier efforts to resolve matters, and trusted my intuition.

I understand the value of open communication and working together—and that was honestly what I thought we had been doing.

I thought that understanding where the actions of the school and the education system were failing to support William and our family would help this system recognise what was going wrong—and that staff would work with us to get it right. I thought feedback would be received and valued.

The "education plan" that had been created as a result of William's determination/diagnosis rarely considered what he needed. In contrast, it considered what the system could deliver in that environment. That was the clear understanding I received from these meetings, and I was now having to insist they looked back at what the plan said he needed and how the school should be meeting it.

After an earlier meeting, I was told that this was the best they could manage for William; it was not perfect, but the best he could hope for.

As the Head of the Autism and Communication "Base" support staff, (also called the "Head of The Base" and the "Communication and Support (C.A.S.) Base") stared out the window in that earlier meeting, I had a feeling he had quietly tried to place William elsewhere, but without success. Having assured me before William started school, with so many platitudes regarding the support available, he was now being made to look foolish because the promised support was not, in fact, being provided to William. When I repeated his words to him, he realised the standard he had promised, and I was calling him out on, had fallen woefully short.

When William "told on them," they denied it. These were often nuanced differences on small events, but they were the warning signs I had missed.

I had to *see* support workers in the act of standing over children who were experiencing meltdowns, to understand where William's perception was coming from. It was exhausting and intensely frustrating to continuously explain what we were observing in William, only to have it ignored or not valued. I raised our concerns that William started in an acoustically unfriendly portacabin. His sensory system began with an overload that may not have been the same as a playground, but it was still highly sensory. In the twenty-first century, children with sensory processing issues (he was not alone) removed their shoes because they did not like the noise inside the portacabin—which they called "the shed"—but this was the dedicated starting place for children with neurodivergence. There was no budget for up-to-standard facilities. Why were the children with sensory difficulties placed in such a sensory room? Surely there was a swap of rooms available? Even this simple solution seemed beyond the support staff abilities. They struggled each day with trying to keep children calm, only to start their day in a room that exacerbated their issues. Yet it did not change.

Illusion of Inclusion

Teachers' comments ranged from the daily complaints of, "Not a good day today, Mrs. Lenormand," and, "He had trouble in the playground again," to, "He threw a piece of puzzle at the teacher and had to be removed from class." He was forced to go home in shame and write a letter of apology to his teacher for that one.

Perspective became absolutely necessary here. Before our experience with William, I would not have questioned a teacher's account. I had never had cause to question my trust in their profession. On this occasion, the teacher gave me so very little information about what had led to the puzzle throwing, that I was forced to ask my son and his support worker to explain.

William said it was getting louder in class and he needed to get away. He had been using a breathing technique to regulate himself through some squealing classroom voices, but it was to little avail. He knew he wanted to shout out, but also knew that was not ok, so he asked his support worker if he could leave. She said that the "Base," the shed he used as an exit space when he was overwhelmed or could not be in the class (too sensory), was in use by another child, so he couldn't go there. This caused him to become too overwhelmed because he felt like there was no escape. Then, as they were tidying up, he did something wrong, his teacher told him off, and he threw a piece of puzzle at her. He was not sure if it hit her because he ran off.

His support worker confirmed he did, indeed, ask to leave and it was unfortunate that they could not provide what he needed at that point—and that *"William must understand this."*

Bless him. He couldn't understand this. William and I discussed explaining this in his letter of apology and requesting whether, maybe, another area could be found outside the classroom, even for a few minutes. I felt like I was doing the obvious thinking for the school staff, and it was extremely frustrating to end my working day and try to resolve theirs too.

When he brought the letter to his headmistress the next day, she took it from him, frowning sternly, and told him off further, in front of me. She didn't even look at the letter or ask what we had discussed at home to try and support him. I couldn't get a word in edgeways. To her, it was simply outrageous that my son would dare to assault one of her teachers who had every right to feel safe at school. I didn't disagree with her sentiment, but this was a far cry from his account and the support worker's. What on earth had the teacher claimed? It lacked some proportionality, at best.

I firmly explained that he had asked to leave because he was getting frustrated and needed time to calm down, and had been refused. The whole point of having a support worker with him was so he could be assisted with his emotions and overwhelming moments. The "Base" was supposed to be the retreat space. I was advised that they had other children in the "Base" that day so he could not go there. There were not enough staff or facilities to extend the support it was recognised that he needed—but that, too, was now his fault, and ours.

As a parent, I know I am not alone in feeling this outraged sense of injustice for my child. But this was a new outrage, caused by their act of shaming him when he had asked for help. I don't imagine the school intended that he would close down, or learn not to ask for help, but that's their lack of awareness of the effect they are having on children in their care.

This situation reminded me of the police service budget cuts—new responsibilities were added, but with no additional staff or training to meet them. It felt very much like a policy direction; the decision to accept neurodivergent children into mainstream schooling had been forced on schools and staff, and they had no real way of meeting it with their existing facilities and experiences. Nor did this teacher have the skill-base required to support him. But, my goodness, they would not be allowed to admit that.

Teachers further crossed boundaries by suggesting we medicate William, which is, ordinarily, a doctor's or medical role. I believe they must have been desperate to find anything to get him to calm down and sit still, but I was so aware of children whose entire personalities changed on these medications that I was reluctant and cautious about using them. The education plan seemed to be sufficient to support him, they just needed to deliver it. I was concerned that medication was a short cut that would, ultimately, not support him in his development. Just round the corner, the Police were forcing entry to premises in an attempt to curb the misuse of prescription medication and psychotropic drugs, but the school staff were now pushing the use of drugs so they could cope with my child in a school setting.

The teaching staff had explained that they had such success with "X" child, who was now taking "Y," (I'm still astounded by the breach of medical confidentiality that was involved here), that they were sure it would help William and he wouldn't be getting into so much trouble. They asked if we could please just go to our doctor and explain why it was needed. And if I didn't find any joy with my doctor—because some physicians don't like to give the medication they suggested—they made it equally clear that they were quite used to supporting parents in wording this request in a way that would ensure it would be fulfilled. They offered to tell me what to say if I needed help getting it through.

The medical guidance we had received was not to medicate a child with William's needs. The medications they referred to are typically used for ADHD-type behaviours, which were predominantly exhibited by William as behaviours due to stress in school. As he aged, the separation of behaviour in home, in other social spaces, and in school became markedly different. ADHD-type behaviours were not evident everywhere. There is no medication for autism, only medications that suppress the symptoms of it.

Too many responses came into my head for me to be able to reply properly. Teaching support giving medical advice—this was wrong! Not to mention their view that I could also be too ignorant to know what to say to a doctor to obtain the prescription on my own, without the educators' help. Were the languages we spoke very different? Yes; Education has a language, and doctors have a language. My child had a language too; he was saying "ENOUGH!" and "I'm struggling here." But he was being ignored.

Our son was eight when this was the consideration. I watched other parents cave to the pressure and insist to medical staff that their child be prescribed medication. I watched the staff and parents collaborate with dutiful reports from the school and educational psychologists, and access to prescriptions were mastered between them. This is less about a presentation of facts at this stage, but of what needs to be said to secure the outcome. No wonder our experience of educational staff was as it was—they complain of parents manipulating a system for support because they do the same.

But is this inclusion? Or support? Or understanding? In reality, the teachers were doing the best they had learned to do with what they had. They were working around a lack of proper resources and spaces, a lack of trained and sufficient staff, and a lack of nurturing environments. They needed our support—through medicating a child—to continue this situation. William was too much for them to manage without medication.

We refused.

I explained that the medication they suggested is classed as a psychotropic drug, and I was not comfortable entertaining anything like it without a doctor telling me it was essential.

Our dealings with medical professionals in this regard could not have been more different, something we also informed the educators of in our numerous meetings. Our GP understood the pressure, but also saw William outside the school environment, and he did not recommend any medication. William's issues with his stomach, often a symptom of anxiety, were reviewed by a paediatric specialist who also understood how hard school was for him. She was a delight to speak to and genuinely understood William and our situation. When she wrote to the school to advise them of the difficulties children with neurodivergence find in a school environment, she received a passive-aggressive letter from the Head of The Base. In his response, he insisted that all provisions were being managed and that the school was going above and beyond, and suggested that the medical professional visit the school to see what a high level of service they were providing. It was clear that the Head of The Base believed we had coloured the doctor's concerns about children with autism in the school.

Her return letter must have been a shock to him as the contents advised him of our complimentary reports of the school's efforts. The specialist thanked him for the offer though and was no doubt left confused by his response. I am sure it surprised him that we could see the cause and the reasons behind it. But the specialist's suggestions were met with the defensive stance we had come to expect from the school. They could not in any way acknowledge that the environment was unsuitable for our son.

The result of our refusal to medicate, in agreement with our doctor's recommendations, was subversive punishment towards our son from his support workers at the school, for behaviours endemic with his age and diagnosis of "ASD and Sensory Processing Disorder." These were exclusions from sports day, school outings, and information about clubs he had an interest in, such as Rugby.

Our own punishment for not conforming as parents was being hauled into meeting after meeting, during working hours, as more and more pressure was applied to get our child to "fit." We experienced being referred to as "mum and dad" in the most patronising terms, with the most basic suggestions being made which indicated a real lack of faith in our ability to parent our child. For example:

Base support worker: "Have you tried supporting him and speaking with him when he says he is worried?"

Me (in my head): No, I bother you every day without thinking of working with him and what he may be worried about.

Base support worker: "Maybe if you behaved like this was a good place for him to be, he would be less worried."

Me (in my head): Sure, I get up every day and tell him that school *is* the horror story he is experiencing and informing me about, but he has to go. I don't spend any time trying to explain his perception, understand what's challenging him, or giving him other explanations. I've almost alienated my son with these efforts to support school!

Base support worker: "He will read if you read to him."

I had no words. Fucking None.

At home we had a breakthrough with William's reading when he explained the words were moving on the page. Eureka! Suspecting some kind of dyslexia, I told the Base support worker that the words were moving and asked how to get him referred for an assessment so he didn't fall behind. She advised the advisory services would not consider this until he was older.

Fortunately, I had the same conversation with the charity that supported us and they suggested that a simple coloured piece of transparent film covering the page could assist. I purchased a selection of yellow, blue, and green film covers online, and placed these over the page. The blue film seemed to settle the words down and he began to read more fluently.

There are many stories from other parents who have circumvented long waits for assessments by doing the research for themselves. It was not the first or last time I was grateful to the autism charities that supported us.

Whilst I can accept that it's worth enquiring about how things are managed at home, schools would do better if they made the inquiry rather than making the assumption that we were doing nothing positive to support William. It was incredibly insulting, and I had a feeling they knew this.

We received condemnation from teachers and support workers, who were all happy to blame a small boy, or his family, for his issues "fitting in."

They glossed over any of our efforts to support him with reading, our offer to be in school to assist, or our additional attendance at autism training. Yves attended extra courses about autism in sports, so he could better support William and other children. At home, we created a sensory room to help William decompress when he came in from school. In an effort to stop him running out of the front door and into the road, we built him a "little house" in the garden for when he needed to get away. Yet it did not suit the school staff to suggest we were supporting him in any way, and at the time I could not fathom why.

On another occasion, the School Nurse contacted us to talk about how she may support William with his anxiety in school, and suggested sessions with a stuffed toy, "Tuck the Turtle." She suggested to William that he could retreat inside the "turtle shell" when he felt bad, rather than lashing out. I explained that at home we were building sensory rooms and, on difficult days, "angry mountains" to give William the space to manage his feelings. I was grateful for her offer as her message was clearly centred around supporting him at home and school. She said she was very surprised by how much effort we were going to. I still wonder why the staff had not informed her, and why her attitude changed so much after this meeting.

It's what teachers have been taught, and I understand, but I chose not to accept it any further. We decided to look at alternatives.

In October 2017, after I drew the line and explained our son was too distressed to attend school, we received the expected calls from the supporting staff, and then the Head of The Base. He could not understand why we had taken this approach. I could not understand how he would think we could do anything else.

Is it really enough to keep complaining and doing nothing? Isn't that the very definition of madness?

I explained that William's distress and the daily teacher complaints clearly showed the "plan" was not working—for anyone. The Head denied this was happening. He said that William was in the best place they could manage for him, and whilst it was not a perfect fit, it was what they would have to do and all that could be offered. Again, I had a feeling he had tried to place him elsewhere and been refused. I explained where William's needs were not being met, that I was receiving constant calls at work to come and get him because they could not manage, and how, as his family, our faith in this being the right place for him felt misplaced. He did not like the push back.

On that day in October 2017, it all came to a head. The new educational psychologist came to our home and explained that she had just moved over to Guernsey from the UK and understood we were at an impasse with the school. The meeting with her went well and it was clear she understood the full situation. She encouraged us to attend a meeting with the support staff and their supervisor to see what we could work out. The words of the new educational psychologist were powerful in our first meeting: "You can insist on William's return to school at once, without accommodation, and it will probably kill him."

Finally, we were seen. The relief we felt was enormous. Finally, someone had stood up to this appalling conduct we had endured from the leader and Head of The Base.

We held fast to our insistence that things needed to change. The Head of The Base refuted that any changes were needed in the educational environment, saying William was already taking up more resources than they had planned. The Head was a manipulative person, a real wolf in sheep's clothing. His smile was passive-aggressive, and my insides churned at his patronising and deceit. He did not appreciate being called out on his department's failings. Both he and his deputy had been informed by me of the things I had witnessed from their staff that they were at pains to disguise.

I complained to his back-office supervisor about his behaviour and was asked to attend a further meeting. As often happens, the complaint was swept away; the supervisor is now leading educational policy. At the time of my complaint, he asked me to be patient as change was coming. The fact I had complained, however, was passed on to the Base staff and the Head of the facility, further straining our relationship.

Naïvely, I thought that our complaint would be taken seriously. I expected it to involve information gathering from all parties, for it to be investigated, and for us to come together afterwards to agree on a direction. Instead, my experience was to receive a label as "one who complains," despite this being the first complaint I had ever made. Despite over a decade with an older child in school. I had never experienced anything like this.

We offered to come into school to assist and support the system as William was reintegrated with the new plan that was put forward by the educational psychologist, but were refused as not having "clearance" for that. At the time, I did not see this red flag. Now, I believe there were simply actions and processes they did not want us to see. They consistently lacked transparency whilst demanding it from us.

I thought they were referring to the required child protection clearances for all people—employees and volunteers—who work with children. We assured the school that we volunteered in a number of places that supported William *and* had child protection clearance. We were former police officers with clear records and over thirty-five years of service between us. In essence, we could produce reports and paperwork to evidence we could be trusted and were endeavouring to demonstrate our commitment to our son and working with the school towards a better plan. If we were there, maybe we would see and understand something that would assist everyone?

The Head of The Base, who was used to manipulating vulnerable people and distressed parents through the inadequacies of the system—and possibly tired of trying to change it—caved in, but was clearly frustrated. We attended the school part-time under strict weekly reviews. He was furious that we had achieved this, and he made no effort to hide it, commenting that William was taking a huge amount of his available staff, time, and resources. Nothing like a bit of resentment to cause an even greater rift in our relationship.

The meetings that followed were, also, often incorrectly documented.

We were forced to keep an eye on the accuracy of the Head's notes and frequently had to challenge the accuracy of his summaries. These were agreed on by everyone else present—until we insisted they had missed very key points. It caused the Head no end of frustration to have to accommodate us with a note keeper for the meetings, as he explained he was "unable to accurately record what had occurred to the standard we required whilst also heading the meetings."

These are the nuances that have a tendency to skew the truth and manipulate information, and he did not like being challenged on his accuracy, preferring to submit his own interpretation at the expense of what was said.

We struggled through until December 2018, when something William had mentioned a lot earlier, came back to us.

The System Strikes Back

Some years earlier, when William first started in the Reception year of the school, he asked me a strange question: "Are things meant to go in bottoms?" I initially figured that, aged four, he had discovered part of his body and was naturally exploring this, but I flagged it with his support worker in case he had heard anything from a classmate they may already have concerns about.

I had absolutely no concerns about William's safety. He rarely went anywhere without us, and never went anywhere without being in a group of other autistic kids during their free play. But a hang-up from my old policing days was that "kids talk." If William had recently been in contact with a "child of concern," they may have said something he was "parroting," so the relevant authorities would need to know. William was four-years-old, so we were still present for bath time and in helping William to clean himself. I was very comfortable that nothing untoward had happened to him so, just in case this comment was led from more-than-normal personal body discovery, I shared it with the school.

From my vantage as an investigator, we are more effective when we work together and, at that stage, I still believed that's what we were doing with full disclosure of all that was happening. I soon found that this was very one-sided. There are signs I am all too familiar with, when a person is subjected to abuse. At school, his support worker dismissed my concern, saying William was often removed or alone and not in contact with other children they had any concerns about. She also made no note of my report.

A few years later, I was safeguarding[1] William with some advice in an effort to prevent him removing his clothes if they were uncomfortable. As he was growing up, it was becoming more of an issue than when he was young. No matter where he was, when his sensory needs took over, off came the trousers and underwear in search of the offending label or seam. This time, it had occurred at an autism support group that was full of understanding parents and people who worked with autism, but I was hoping to avoid it happening in more public places. I can just imagine the judgey "parenting advice" from random strangers, and the pointing fingers of William's peer group who did not need to remove their clothes because of a label. Other children tended to laugh, but as William and his peers aged, I was concerned that this would be less funny and more harmful to his social relationships. I explained to William, "What is in your pants is private. We keep bottoms and willies hidden from public view, so people don't like it if you start suddenly stripping off. They don't understand why you are doing that."

All he said in response was that, "bottoms are disgusting." I understood him to be referring to the place poo comes from, as that had been the source of much upset at school with his anxious-tummy response, and had been exacerbated by a comment from his support worker—in front of him—that he had experienced diarrhea "and it smelled very bad." He was always embarrassed to be sent home with an upset tummy and had now connected that his "bottom was disgusting" in the same way he had connected that it was "easier to die than just keep not understanding."

A few days after our safeguarding chat, as is often the case with William and the way he processes information, he asked me again if "things went in bottoms?" This time, while we were parked outside the school waiting for the time to go in,

---

1. In this context, I refer to understanding when a child is at a stage where their safety may be compromised by their behaviours, and using appropriate language and examples to help them understand this.

I asked him why he asked that question. William spoke to me about contact he had experienced with another child of his age that amounted to clothes off and some exploration of what was where. It seemed perfectly innocent but I needed to explore this a bit further, and not whilst rushing to school. So I removed him for the day by going into The Base and advising his support worker that I was concerned about what he had said, and wanted to make some enquiries relating to this comment. I was going to keep him with me and take the day off work. I also reminded her of his earlier statement from a few years before.

His support worker denied all knowledge of the earlier statement, which concerned me because I had reported his words directly to her. Immediately, she ushered me into a cupboard and, as she shut the cupboard door behind me, she asked—in hushed tones—what had happened. I was upset by her behaviour and denial of the earlier knowledge and wanted to get back to my son, without panic, and review his comments safely and without rushing. I certainly did not want to be in a cupboard.

I honestly thought she would understand me to be a professional investigator, a mother who was reasonably "checking" the information and that, particularly because of my police training, I was qualified to do so. If I found anything suspect, I knew exactly what to do with it.

I had no reason at all to lie to the school about what had been said, and it never occurred to me to keep it to myself. I placed a high standard of trust in them by being completely open about the situation, only to watch them inaccurately record and bastardise the information to a point that, like their meeting notes, it was almost unrecognisable as the same event.

What they recorded here was something else. The headmistress called me, and I challenged their record immediately. I let her know that we had also been working with CAMHS (Child and Adult Mental Health Services) following our dogged insistence on support, despite their first response that they don't work with kids with autism.

The CAMHS specialist also called a meeting with the school, to correct their position as it was being relayed incorrectly. The specialist was told by the Head of The Base that she had held the wrong type of meeting, so what she said could not be actioned!

Again the Head of The Base found a way to bastardise a process to suit his insistence that a member of staff from MASH (Multi Agency Support Hub) would be seeing me to ensure a team was placed around William to safeguard him. His friend and colleague would lead the team as I was not confident in him and could see him working around the impending complaint he knew would be coming, again, about his conduct and misrecording of important information. I insisted on knowing why the Head felt William was unsafe. He refused to say. So I refused to engage with the idea without some clarity around why it was necessary.

The school saw me, and treated me, as a royal pain, simply for holding them to their motto: "Every child. Every chance. Every day.", and their educational plan for our son, while also pointing out where their actions flew in the face of it. Parents who make themselves this kind of nuisance about the safeguarding and welfare of their children are rarely a risk to them. However, the actions of the Head of The Base suggested that we were now being considered a risk to William.

Enter our horror story.

A further meeting was called, but that morning William became unwell with shingles. As usual, I notified the school and explained why William would not be attending that day. At home, I started to make arrangements for some cover care for him, as I knew we were required at the meeting and I was determined to see this properly documented and not further misrepresented. William's Nan was able to step in to look after him for a few hours.

The strangest events followed my phone call to the school.

For the first time, I received a telephone call from a School Attendance Officer, who declined to share her name, but asked that I provide evidence from the doctor that William had shingles. What a strange request. I was familiar with the need for "sick notes" for work, but I had never been asked for a sick note for a child.

It also cost fifty pounds to go to a doctor at that time, as only private healthcare is available in the Channel Islands. After months of reduced pay, reduced hours at work due to needing to care for William and attend these additional meetings, our budget was tight. I explained that I did not need to spend this, and that to my knowledge there was nothing to do for shingles that we could not cover in caring for him ourselves. I thought the request was unusual and asked the Attendance Officer why it was being made as there was no issue, in my awareness, in regards to William's attendance. She agreed there had not been any issue with his attendance but asked that he was taken to the doctor anyway. It was so vague, I think I could have justifiably treated it as a crank call.

I replied, however, that if the school was insisting on it, then they should pay for it. She confirmed the Education Department would pay the bill, so I dutifully took William to the doctor to confirm he did have shingles and that my treatment plan of time away from school and treating him with kids' Nurofen® to manage any pain he complained of would be more than sufficient.

Yves and I made it into school—with the doctor's note—in time for our scheduled meeting. The staff appeared surprised to receive the doctor's note, and equally surprised that we were there for the planned meeting. William did not attend these summons, just us. Why would they think we would not make plans for him?

I realised they had quietly orchestrated this request for a doctor's note in the belief they would catch me in a lie because they thought I was trying to avoid the meeting. Not satisfied, they advised me that they had cancelled the meeting with us—without informing us—*and* had held the meeting without us because they had not expected us to attend. It was then that we discovered the School Attendance Officer was the wife of the Head of The Base. Instead of clarifying if we could attend the meeting, he had called his wife to insist that we provide proof of his shingles diagnosis because he felt we were trying to avoid the meeting.

We had attended every event, every meeting, and every phone call they had required of us. Yet again, the Head was trying to manipulate events to suggest we would avoid a meeting or lie about our son's state of health. What I did not yet know was why?

Finally, his personal views were fully revealed—and the basis with which he held them was unfounded. He made no effort to enquire if we would be attending the meeting in light of William's illness, but went to covert lengths to try to prove some level of dishonesty on our part, no doubt in the belief it would strengthen his case. To me, it provided evidence of the wilful blindness we experienced from him, as well as from several of the supporting staff at the school. The situation was becoming increasingly dangerous. These kinds of allegations, especially when kept behind closed doors and whispered about, can cause significant harm—and I was done with their behaviour.

To make matters even clearer for us, the School Attendance Officer, the Head of The Base's wife, then denied ever making the phone call or request! Fortunately, it was recorded by the doctor's surgery and on my phone when I received the call, and the headmistress agreed, irregular as it was, to view the evidence presented to her and pay the doctor's fee. At this point, she also seemed to be questioning the information she was being given.

I called my previous police supervisor, who had a background in child protection, to establish who was the head of MASH, so I could speak with them and establish if what the Head of The Base had said was true about his right to demand a safeguarding team be placed around William, and if there was any way I could find out what he was up to. After I explained how worried I was about the system being manipulated like this, she empathised. In our line of work, we had both seen manipulation and had to fight against it. But this time, I was bearing the brunt of being on the "other side."

When I telephoned MASH, I asked for my call to be returned by the supervisor, explaining that I wished to complain about someone acting in their agency's name. The Head of The Base had suggested—twice—that he had a long-established connection with Children's Services, and he was insisting that William was unsafe. I felt it best to talk to the person in charge of MASH, to stop the "Chinese Whispers" and theorising, and work directly with Children's Services. Unfortunately, the message got muddled at their end and was intercepted by another social worker.

She did not disclose that she had already been contacted by the Head of The Base in supporting William. Instead, she feigned ignorance of any information relating to us and explained that the person I was seeking was unavailable. She asked to visit me at home, which I naively agreed to, so that she could explain to me what a "team around the child" service involved. I was part of William's support team and was looking forward to the idea that there may be additional support we could tap into in regard to his schooling.

In no way did my experience of working with social workers in the police prepare me for the way this visit progressed. Again, I had a level of expectation that we would be working together to resolve matters.

Once in my home, however, the social worker sat in our lounge making polite conversation about children and autism, before explaining that she had accessed some concerning information about my older child having been abused. She was concerned that I had "two children who had been abused," and was seeking to assess us as a family.

The room swam. I was being ambushed by a volume of incorrect and inaccurate information, and the injustice raged within me. I explained to her that the information about our eldest son was well within my knowledge; it was a vicious allegation made by his father during our divorce that had been investigated in full and proven unfounded. Her records should reflect this. The family involved in his allegation had experienced significant harm as a result of his accusation. They had been in the process of adopting two children in need, and it was halted due to the controlling and purely speculative allegation. To use that, proven false, information to approach William some ten years later was an abuse and bastardisation of that information. I was sickened to my stomach regarding what was being manipulated here—and I told her so.

When leaving, the social worker explained to me, in my hallway, that I could either comply with their insistence that I name the other child involved with William, or face the consequences of answering to the Children's Board. For now, they were "parking" William's diagnosis of autism and, instead, considering him a child at risk of harm, as his "behaviours" could be evident of that. Suddenly, they had decided he was a child being harmed in the home. She also said she would be presenting these findings in a meeting the following day.

I felt the Lion, Bear, *and* Wolf mothers rise within me in defence of my cub. How I didn't snarl at her through my teeth, at her threat to my family, I do not know. My feelings were entirely primal and I fought down my fury at these manipulated wrongs.

As an aside, if a diagnosis is in doubt, there is a method by which it can be revisited. Reassessment can be requested. No authority has the right to simply "park" an inconvenient truth. If she felt my children were at risk, why did she not see them and check them, there and then, for herself. They were readily available to her.

But it was all a smoke screen.

I advised her that I would attend that meeting with the full information in hand, and not allow her to present a half-cocked piece of information that deliberately distorted the truth. She advised me I had "no right" to be present at the meeting, that it was for professional staff only, but she would pass on my "threat" to attend. It was laughable that she was threatening me in my home, yet would suggest that my anger at her manipulation was threatening.

She did not offer to check her information or research it further in light of the detailed information I gave her. Nothing. She was going to override a long medical diagnosis and make a spurious assumption without any evidence, purely because I could see no valid reason for naming a child in a non-incident, and I had given her evidenced and valid reasons as to why.

The fact she felt threatened by me even suggesting I would be attending with the full information was also incredibly telling. If that is not being "suppressed" by a system, I do not know what is. I told her the accusations and situation were "outrageous," and she left the house. They also ignored their own published policy—to include the family in all meetings—without any explanation as to why.

William had been a child in need of support since before he started school. He needed a team around him, and we had been fighting for that since the first allegations that he was unwelcome in a school environment were raised. Heck, truth be told, we all could have used some support as a family. But no matter what we tried, it didn't appear for us, other than from the volunteer sector who have supported countless families through similar events.

Nothing had changed.

> *Nothing had, in fact, happened to William, but the people supposed to support him decided—without basis—not to believe me, not to support us, and we were left wondering why.*

We were denied access to the professional meeting to speak for ourselves, and denied the opportunity to present anything to them. That's the abuse that can be caused by the processes they safeguard. These abuses take place behind closed doors and in secret.

The school broke up for Christmas and we went to England to take a well-earned rest with my parents. During this time, there was no contact made with us and no messages left for us in any way, so I was surprised to return to work after the Christmas break to discover that police enquiries had been instigated because I had refused to engage with the social worker—who was a "friend" of the Head of The Base.

I asked when I had refused? She had been in my house. How was I refusing to engage? I had wanted to attend the meeting. I asked about the concerns they had and was left none the wiser as to why a child contact matter between two children the same age—something I would ordinarily have managed, without question, in my earlier role as a police officer—was now being questioned. When did we become "unsafe?"

The truth we later uncovered was that a staff member at The Base was concerned that my eldest son was nine years older than William, and she wondered what William might be subjected to. She made comments about the computer games William was witnessing. I explained that he knew the names of the games but was not in the room where his brother played. Like most young boys, he bragged about the names but if they asked him, he would not know much about the game beyond a very basic summary. In October 2018, some family background research was instigated, based on her comments, by the Head of The Base, using his contacts at MASH. He could find no trace of an elder brother. The email exchange I uncovered between them seemed to take some covert questioning to establish that our eldest son has a different surname. This search revealed that there was an old allegation from our eldest son's father.

My disclosure about simple child contact had caused them to link this information, incorrect and incomplete as it was, to place our eldest child firmly under the spotlight. No amount of character references and teacher contacts from our eldest son's school to explain that they had no concerns, that others working with him had no concerns, that a placement service for children receiving off-island education that worked closely with us had no concerns, were able to halt this assumption. My insistence that they had incomplete information also did not stop their assumptions. They did not check the information. Nor did the Police Officer with full access to it.

It was an utter shambles, felt completely malicious, and we were forced to ride the waves of error after error as they bypassed all accepted investigative and safeguarding practices.

Responding to the Strike Against Us

Over the coming weeks, I took additional support with me into meetings: two third party representatives, one from the charity, NAS Guernsey (National Autistic Society, Guernsey) and the other a concerned States Deputy, a politician who represents the people. I went as high as I could to try and get some sense into this situation as they derailed the entire process of any child protection enquiry. These representatives had both known us for some time and could refute the unevidenced and harmful claims coming from the Head and his team. It was my intention that they would witness the horror and manipulation we were enduring—and help me change it.

The States Deputy offered her support, saying she was quite shocked at their response to her presence in the meeting. I was given a verbal "dressing down" for not telling the other attendees that I would be bringing support in the form of a States Deputy. On top of this, the Head of The Base pulled our support person from NAS Guernsey to one side, to explain to her that he wished to, "get past the fact that William had an autism diagnosis and concentrate on his concerns."

She advised him (and later informed me), that if the Head of Services felt the diagnosis of medical professionals was incorrect, he should appeal it with evidence. He never did this. Teachers have the capacity to contest medical evidence if they disagree with it, or to ask for a reassessment of a child, as they are not medically qualified to reassess autism. They are valued for their observations, which can be reviewed by medical professionals, but they need to work together to revisit a diagnosis.

The school never did any of this. Their actions just didn't add up and we couldn't understand what was happening—or why.

Then there was the police. In my twenty years of working as an officer involved in many investigations, I was a service to my community, but in the later years, it changed shape from a police *service* to a police *force*. This one word change altered the entire ethos of policing for me. "Force" implies you will do as you are told. There are definitely moments when this is necessary, where officers hold or draw a line for valid reasons of safety and community. "Service" implies that we work together, that I serve my community by asking questions and restoring the quality of life they are seeking. Service is something you can trust as a standard, that you can call upon for help. I needed the police service, but met the police force in the shape of a truly awful officer. I was embarrassed by the sheer lack of integrity of the investigating police officer. She never thought to question why a teacher was giving "expert medical opinion," or why he was not seeking a review of the medical diagnosis. Her actions stank more of a personal grudge, and the fact there was simply not one shred of evidence to support anything they claimed left us to conclude little else.

Her telephone calls, and those of her supervisors, were equally embarrassing. They shared nothing of their inquiry, listened to nothing we said, made threats that "this is not going away," and kept demanding the family's name to repeat history. I couldn't do it. I am part of a service, and could see no service to my community by setting anyone else up for a railroad of a show that was as far removed from an evidence-based investigation as I have ever seen.

Her case hinged on my lack of support, but mainly on my refusal for them to go fishing about my eldest son without a shred of evidence that William had been harmed in any way. She asked why I would not name the child involved so they could check for themselves. I explained that she should verse herself with the substantial records and complaints dated and made at the police station a decade earlier in relation to the abuse allegations from our eldest son's father. Due to the fact that the family in that case had been caused significant harm by their approach, I wasn't prepared to open another family to abuse when nothing had happened and nothing had, apparently, changed in the police approach—akin to the abuse we were already suffering.

In true "bully-boy" fashion, my refusal to name the other poor child in this innocent and, so far, harmless event, or hand them or their family up to save ourselves, placed my husband and me in front of the Safeguarding Children's Panel.

A few days before this serious event, a new social worker had been appointed to us, and she only had others' sworn testimony to go on at that time. The police officer gave evidence that she had conducted enquiries—that she had not conducted—saying there was no history of information that I referred to with the allegation regarding our eldest son. Essentially, she gave false evidence. The Head of The Base gave evidence that he felt William's diagnosis of autism should be "parked" in favour of considering that he was being abused—and again, no one questioned it.

The meeting also started in the most hostile way. My husband advised the school nurse that she had not spelled our name correctly on the official paperwork she was filing. He was simply asking for a correction when she spat at him that it was not her fault, that she was dyslexic and not good with spelling.

Based on no information or evidence offered in the meeting, and to the horror of our supporting officer, a Child Protection order was passed. We were *required* to engage with the social worker, something we had offered to do from the start. Our door had been open and they had made visits, but they wanted to make more. No one was denying them access. There was no need for this order, other than it being another way to bully us.

My husband and I were totally destroyed. Then, as the snarky Police Officer left the room, she commented over her shoulder with a smile, "You are taking this personally, aren't you?" No one questioned this either.

I needed to review and question this quickly, so I looked forward to receiving the minutes I was assured were being taken by the lady in the corner of the room. When we received them, many weeks later, it was with a covering apology that they were not very full or complete. The person taking the minutes had little training and not all remarks or comments had been recorded. The "notes" bore little semblance to what was said and represented more of a convenient summary than an accurate record. The notes also reflected that we had *volunteered* to be placed under a Child Protection Order. Again, our independent support shook his head in disbelief, as did we.

The social worker turned out to be rather wonderful and, at least, had some understanding of our child's needs. Two months and a few meetings later, we were back reporting to the Child Protection Panel where, this time, we insisted on the meeting being audio recorded. They accommodated my "unusual" request because of the issues that appeared in the inaccurate recording of the last meeting.

The Police Officer had been removed from further proceedings, and there was no representation from the police service at all. This is strange as they had given the most insistent statement. Why were the police not represented at all? Why no explanation?

The Head of The Base was also not present.

Something had happened in the background that no one was speaking about.

The Child Protection Order was spoken of as if it was something we had *volunteered* to enter into, rather than something forced upon us in a shameful way. Thankfully, it was lifted in record time. I suspect a review revealed the sheer lack of evidence and abuse of authority we suffered. But that was kept very quiet and well away from any admission to us.

There was no concern for William. The order was removed and no one commented as to why it had ever been necessary.

What On Earth Do We Do Now?

We had been unable to stop this happening to us, and were so shocked and horrified that this could happen to anyone that Yves and I decided to start our own investigation. We both needed to work out how on earth this had happened and ensure it never happened again. I had not heard or witnessed anything like it and it fell so far short of any service either of us anticipated or believed was there. We had begun to review the entire situation following the requirement to take William to the doctor regarding shingles. We could not afford an advocate or solicitor to trawl through the volume of material we were going to need to explore, so we requested the information and did it ourselves.

We sought access to our own data, or any data concerning us, via a Subject Access Request, which all people have access to as a right enshrined in the Data Protection (Guernsey) Law, or respective laws governing the protection of your personal data in other countries. We required all records held about us and our children in an effort to understand how this was allowed to happen and ensure it couldn't happen again. Because of our service background and community values, neither my husband nor I wanted to consider that anyone else would have to endure a situation like this.

The Data Protection (Guernsey) Law (or "Act" in the UK) and their equivalents, were passed in many countries to safeguard your right to be forgotten and to oversee how your personal data is managed and used. Data held about you should be correct and you have the right to view it to ensure it is. In our case, very old information had been manipulated and was incorrect which led to suggest a pattern of abuse—that should never have been allowed to happen. The full information was not exchanged, only a snippet which then skewed the context. Had it been exchanged in full, this could not have occurred. The police officer tasked with finding and producing it suggested it did not exist, although she had some personal knowledge of the matter.

Reviewing the records took time and they had to be gathered from different government departments. Firstly from the Education Department, which needed to be chased for the records over several months, and reminded of the records they held. There was a substantial amount of missing information. Health Services produced their records, as did the Police who, as they often do, heavily redacted their information. Redactions can only be made in certain circumstances, and they can be challenged.

Today, I hear from so many parents of children undergoing the trauma of this malpractice. Some get the same answer we did: Lessons have been learned.

This is a phrase I'm tired of hearing. It's like apologising without context.

If something has been "learned," the least we deserve to know is: *What was learned? What was not obvious at the outset to the party who learned this lesson? Is it reasonable to believe that they did not have this knowledge initially and only learned this after a situation occurred?* History is littered with examples of what should have been obvious at the outset:

- The R.M.S *Titanic* was famously touted as "unsinkable." But the basic principle of ensuring enough lifeboats were on board for everyone should have been a priority, regardless of how advanced or "unsinkable" the ship was assumed to be.

- Leading up to the 2008 global financial crash, banks issued subprime mortgages to people who were unlikely to repay them. This occurred at a time when lending large sums to individuals with poor credit histories was clearly unsustainable.

My point is that ignoring fundamental issues, or taking risks and finding ways around the law or procedures in favour of expediency or overconfidence, can lead to catastrophic consequences.

A short while later, a new Facebook group appeared for Guernsey. It was created to gather parents' experiences with social services in the area—because another family felt the service could not be trusted. The public had turned to social media in an effort to get the information out there. Whilst Yves and I preferred to conclude our investigation ourselves rather than over social media, we were aware that more families came forward and that, suddenly, we were not alone in being accused in this way.

In autism literature and educational psychology reviews and books, we can clearly see the abuse of vulnerable people within a system that is ill-equipped to manage the challenges.

Even the police officer could not understand why I would not allow her to interview William without some autism training. It's so easy to read his type of communication incorrectly. You would not speak to another person in a different language without admitting you need an interpreter.

The investigative practice of shutting out parents of neurodivergent children without strong evidence to do so needs to cease, but I'm sad to see in recent reports from Guernsey that it continues.

I am thankful our social worker saw and asked about the dynamic between the investigating officer and myself. She also noted that the officer was happy for me to be present when she questioned our eldest son, aged seventeen, but not with our youngest. I explained to her that I had avoided this officer whilst I was in the police service as our views on "service to the public" differed widely. The investigating officer embodied "force" whereas I preferred "service."

It was not lost on the social worker how much this officer had enjoyed marching into our home in the most inappropriate way, making accusations, and scratching her high heels across our flooring, then saying, "Sorry, did you want me to take my shoes off?"

I felt betrayed by a service I had been part of and trusted to protect us from these kinds of wrongs, a service that did nothing to safeguard the interest of my child, or the public, from this type of abuse of positional behaviour. If they seriously thought William was at risk from me, why was he still with me? If they thought anyone in the family would hurt him, why would he still be there? Their actions and decisions made no sense if they honestly held these views or beliefs.

By not questioning the actions of the Head of The Base in time, this service did nothing to protect my family from abuse. How can a teacher supersede medical evidence provided to them? It's evidentially unsound. They sought medical evidence for a shingles diagnosis that required a child to miss school for a few days, but wanted to ignore a protracted and lengthy medical assessment of autism when it did not suit them.

Our Data Protection request revealed the shocking emails exchanged between education authorities, child psychologists, and other professionals. These documents were almost unbelievable and led to a startling outcome—the Head of The Base resigned immediately and returned to the UK with his wife. He saw what was coming and ran away.

His abrupt departure effectively stopped any further questions being asked of him, and I had to work hard to gather the traces of any material he had left behind. He destroyed, or took, a substantial amount of it. Records showed that in the months preceding my approach to the school regarding William, there was a covert collaboration between the Head of The Base, some staff members, and social services. They had decided to "park" our young son's diagnosis and, instead, allege that he was being abused at home. My transparency about William's conversation with another child allowed them to mask their actions, but the timeline of events exposed the deceit. The police investigation, had there been one, should have revealed this.

Our request for records was breaking down the system, revealing its inadequacies, and upsetting those who were trying to hide within it. The Head of The Base could not admit his inability to help or support William in school, nor could he justify why they failed to meet his needs, as outlined in their own plan. Lies were used to protect the system; this was difficult to stomach and highlighted the overpowering pressure for everyone to conform.

It took significant effort to bring these lies to light. Data Protection Laws provided us with the necessary documentation, but I still wonder what was said to the Head of The Base that prompted his swift resignation soon after our request was filed. Such covert operations by services erode community trust.

If there had been genuine concern for William's wellbeing, why was he left in our care? If there were no doubts about our safeguarding abilities, why act so subversively? These contradictory actions undermine any sincere concern regarding child protection and safeguarding, which makes a mockery of the entire system.

Whilst The Base staff left and "went sick," we stayed on and worked to repair the harm. Our son continued in school in the hopes that their motto of "Every child. Every chance. Every day." would bear some fruit with the arrival of a new Head. It didn't work out, but that was not because we did not try.

I believe lessons can be learned. Some of them are bloody obvious from the start, and some take time to embed. Some children are suited to the current educational system, some are not, and it has always been here as an issue, which is now amplified because we have been ignoring it. Just because a schooling environment is a fit for *some* children, does that *have* to be true for all children? Can we offer something better than torture, to those whom it does not fit?

What William Did Next

Without the overt control of the former Head of The Base, we could see more clearly what William was finding difficult about his school environment.

The following school year saw a new teacher for William. Put simply, she was exceptional.

She understood where he was struggling, noticed his cues, and advised me that she was concerned about the way the support staff tried to take him out of class at the slightest event. She was a highly experienced teacher who managed a wide range of needs in the classroom and playground with apparent ease. She was encouraging, supportive, and firm with him, but understood that he was trying and had yet to find his method. William flourished beautifully under her guidance.

The Base was not done though, and one afternoon I answered the phone at work to discover it was William's support worker. There had been an incident and she wanted to know who was collecting William. As I had altered my working hours to always be the one to pick him up from school, I was confused by the question but confirmed that it would be me.

I was instructed to make sufficient time at collection to attend a meeting about William's conduct that day.

As the other children left, William was waiting for me in the classroom with his head bowed, obviously unhappy. Clearly, he had been told off. I sat next to him and asked what had happened.

The support worker spoke through gritted teeth as she explained his "appalling" behaviour. Whilst changing for P.E., William had whipped off his shorts and waved his private parts around with a few of the other boys. (In our earlier investigation, they had denied ever seeing evidence of William removing his clothes in school like this, but there it was, again.)

I noted the other parents and children had no meeting but, at that moment, William's exceptional teacher entered the room and asked what was going on. She said, "If you have made a big deal out of silly boy conduct today, I think that's overly ridiculous." I could have kissed her; I could not have said it better myself. Here was yet another example of this so-called support staff overreaching child behaviour with sexualised conduct.

We developed a better relationship with the head teacher following this fallout. Once she understood our concerns and the high level of engagement we had with both our children, she thawed and was supportive in further meetings. It may have taken a while, but I appreciated that she had relied on her staff for accurate information that she was now starting to question.

William continued in his need for change, and continued to struggle to follow instruction and manage the social conditions around him. It is a lot to ask of the current system, teachers, children, and their parents, to support the idea that this was the "best" place for him. The following school year had a different teacher, and when I picked him up, I heard that he had a difficult day. I do believe it was difficult for everyone.

We engaged with the school in a programme called *The Decider Skills*[1] which helped children understand their emotions. Along with William, we attended after-school classes that he appeared to thoroughly enjoy. Seeing his Mum and

---

1. *The Decider Skills* uses Cognitive Behaviour Therapy to teach children, young people and adults the skills to recognise their own thoughts, feelings and behaviours, enabling them to monitor and manage their own emotions and mental health.

Dad perched on little school chairs really pleased him.

The parents invited to attend were there to help their children recognise emotions and choose responses. As per my earlier suggestion to the school nurse, we were finally in agreement with the school that it was useful to employ the same language when trying to support the children.

It transpired that the local schools had received information from a recent study that indicated the mental health of junior school children (UK age four-to-eleven, and neurotypical, as we understand it) had been assessed as being at epidemic levels of depression and anxiety.

It's not only neurodivergent children who are pushing back at the way the school system is set up, or being affected by it. As such, the school William attended had identified some children who may benefit from learning about their inner "fizz" in *The Decider Skills* course.

Good grief. I'm grateful for the study, and that someone took the time to do it, but most of us with eyes can see that a significant number of children are NOT happy at school.

This example is akin to the bland statement of "Lessons have been learned." It's a common phrase in the UK, from politicians to directors of companies and most States of Guernsey departments. Most complaints result in the suggestion that a lesson has been learned.

What was learned that wasn't obvious to everyone else? How many times did it happen before the lesson was "caught" by the investigation? Again, is it reasonable that they did not know in the first place?

The Decider Skills course started a new thought process for me.

What if our kids were able to learn about themselves and their emotions before they learned about what they were interested in?

Or at the very least, what if they had a great deal more focus on this valuable knowledge, that currently exists as an addendum to the standard curriculum.

Could this bridge the gap between school and the workplace? Between children and their mental health?

Could we prepare them best for life by all working towards helping each child understand themselves first.

Can we then value them all for the uniqueness they bring to the world?

In school, our son was not learning anything he needed. But he was learning lessons that led him to show significant signs of doubting his self-worth and natural abilities. He was doubting his ability to be resilient, and to develop areas that were tricky for him because he did not get it "right" the first time in tests.

His reluctance to try new things was due to a rapidly shrouding fear of not being able to get it right; in the school environment he was unable to understand that we learn through *trying* and *practice* to get it right in the end.

At that point, I surrendered to my inner knowing: William is not here to "fit."

The education system was no longer a "fit" for how we lived and worked.

And I became ok with this concept.

I chose change.

To keep trying was killing his soul, the core of who he was.

In a cry recognised by mothers across the globe, I knew I would do anything to protect my children. But it took watching his soul shrivel in value for me to fully understand.

Up to that point, he did not know how to value himself any more than I did.

I finally recognised that I was viewing everything through the wrong lens. It wasn't for him to "fit" with school; school was not a "fit" for him.

This was not quitting.

This was identifying with his actual needs and the gifts he genuinely has to bring to the world, to discover for himself what he wanted. He had his own magic; the magic of "Not Fitting."

This approach was described to me as "child-led learning."

I don't mind telling you that I had quite a few sleepless nights as I started to look at other "not fitting" ways of raising our children. At first, I felt feverish just thinking of leaving the system this way. How on earth would we manage? How do I work and school him? Pay for the house? What the heck does this look like? These questions kept me up and disturbed my sleep, again…

It's one thing to realise you are through with the "old ways" and quite another to figure out what to do next—and actually do it.

It was one thing to realise our son's needs would not be met by traditional schooling methods—but how would I meet them?

Was I really going to do a better job?

I'd trained police officers, taught Law in classrooms to student officers, and taught them to apply diverse skills—but could I teach my son, who resisted so much? He was loud at playtime, and highly agitated by the presence of other children. Unless they were playing his game his way, he appeared to have no ability to be flexible in play.

And he was big!

Strong.

"Doesn't know his own strength," my mum said. That was true!

Just before he was diagnosed with autism, William was angry with me for not allowing him access to something. I can't remember what it was, but it was probably food. He ate all the time. It was hard to manage his voracious appetite and I suspected that, like a baby, he was receiving sensory comfort from food in his mouth.

He would never accept a pacifier or dummy, though. A garden snail, however, was fine—until he vomited.

The reason I mention his strength is that on one occasion during this time, when he was highly agitated, he grabbed my right little finger. His little face was all screwed up and red with anger. It hurt. I was surprised at his strength. I told him so and asked him to let go. He tweaked it harder and bent it further backwards, such was his agitation. I cried out and shouted for him to stop—then he asked if it would break? Calm as you like, still red-faced, he spoke with curiosity, not malice.

I assured him it probably would, as it was already throbbing, and said he should let go. I twisted my finger against his thumb in his grip—the way I'd been trained in the police service to exit a hold on me—feeling quite ridiculous to have to do this with my young son. But the grip of this three-year-old boy did not budge. I was a long way from comfortable in giving him the recommended police "distraction strike," but it was so painful that I honestly thought about it just before he let go.

My finger was sprained from his efforts, and it took a few weeks for the pain to subside. I remember thinking that he was ridiculously strong for his age, and that teaching him self-control was an absolute must.

Recalling this was not helping me to move forwards. In fact, it was keeping me stuck in my fears about trying something different.

At that time, he was a product of confusion. I was parenting in a hurry, trying to extra explain things and still make time for work, which was a lot of additional pressure. William was doing things he did not want in places he could not manage. However, home education can look different and I was no longer bringing the same things to the table with my juggling act, so it made sense that what he would bring was also likely to alter.

I've taught people how to face their fears. I've been that support for others, but my biggest breakthrough happened when I realised:

Just try it. Feel your way through. It doesn't HAVE to be absolutely right off the bat. You are both going to learn what's needed as you go.

Ok—great. That's the teaching worry tackled.

The Transformation Choice

What about the money?

What changes could we make to ease that situation? Most months, our income matched our outgoing expenses, so that definitely needed a review.

What could we do without?

We downsized and replaced our two cars with one electric vehicle. This saved fuel costs, insurance for one vehicle, and put money back in the bank.

Growing our own vegetables, slow cooking, and reducing the amount of fast food and pre-prepared supermarket goods (Good grief, that's expensive stuff), saved me hundreds of pounds a month on my shopping bill. I was honestly surprised at how expensive convenience had become.

We sold furniture and all the extras we did not need: bikes the boys had grown out of, clothes, books, musical instruments, and unused tools.

I reduced my hours at work, which then cost me my senior position—was this punishment for not "sucking it up" any longer? Then I resigned. I don't owe anyone loyalty that does not match my own.

As this happened, so did the global COVID-19 pandemic. My in-laws moved in with us just as the world shut down; with an apparent sixth sense, I believe they were seeking to restructure their living support. Their family home was no longer something they could manage as it was full of damp and needed a lot of work they did not want to do. There were also real fears as the position of their house, situated on the high side of a hill, meant there were steep steps and their home was having an effect on my father-in-law's health.

The family pitched in, and my in-laws decided to distribute proceeds from the sale of their house to each of their sons. They tried living with us as extended family for a while, but after the pandemic, it wasn't what they wanted. They were miserable, and couldn't find a way to be happy with the changes, so they moved out.

With their support though, we were able to clear our credit cards and debts, until we were left with only the mortgage. We wondered, "Ok, what's the next step now?"

Part III. A New Beginning

Our eldest son, George, was heading to university in Scotland. He had made it to his dream course placement and could not wait. This meant that the house was too big for only the three of us.

We had tried renting rooms to students, but it was unsettling for William. At one point, having cared for other children needing support, we thought about fostering. Again, there was too much concern about how William would feel sharing his home and his family in the long-term. It was not something we felt we could "try" as that would potentially be unfair on a child hoping to be placed.

We also lived on a small island and, while there was a solid home education community, for a child who preferred to learn "hands on" like our son, it became a bit repetitive. I had worked out that he did not have much interest in the things I had tried with him. He did engage with us and that was far better than school—but that didn't mean we were exactly where we needed to be... yet.

It was also unreliable and prohibitively expensive to keep travelling off-island for new experiences. It looked like we had outgrown Guernsey. So, we flipped the focus again and rented out our house. The rental market was buoyant and the house was large and well kept.

Taking William out of his familiar space was going to be challenging. He needed his home, his room, and space to decompress. He loved to shut the big front door behind him.

I had a small moment of brilliance when I wondered how I could take a home with us, picturing a snail needing to withdraw into its shell—and with that we moved into our motorhome, timing our eldest son's university start date with our new life, and established *Adventures In Learning*. What better way to support our young son than to give him the closeness and security of both parents being right alongside him as he learned to embrace change, work through fear and anxieties, and discover himself and what he loves?

It's also a *far* cheaper way of living on a budget.

The only stumbling block was having our two dogs—both very active and bouncy cocker spaniels who lived outside and would be most unhappy travelling in a motorhome. With the help of friends, we made enquiries to see if there was a better option for them. I sobbed as they jumped into the back of their new family's car a few months later. They behaved as if they had always been there, with two older dogs to keep them company too.

"Van life" is being embraced by so many people who are enjoying the freedom brought by living outside "four walls." Some have moved in out of necessity, through separations and loss of homes but, in doing so, have discovered a whole new way of living.

We chose it as a way to support our son through life skills and learning. We have met other families who have done the same, with pets and children of various ages and needs, for a variety of reasons. New work popped up in the three years that followed. Promising possibilities to support the community and address injustices and imbalance. These were very common themes amongst the people we met in our travels. But most ideas didn't get off the ground. And some financially wealthy individuals were utterly dishonest, taking as much as possible from those who were desperate to see change around Health, Justice, and Education. These people brought little but harm to those whose support they took.

But all experiences were helping us learn something new.

Three years later, the pensions we had contributed to during our working lives were being paid, and we loved the life we had reimagined—so much that we sold the house in Guernsey and entered our fiftieth year of life mortgage free and debt free.

We did not need to see a doctor at all in that time, whereas before this change, we had been fairly regular surgery visitors with all manner of colds and injuries.

We now have a small home in Scotland as a base, where we embrace the outdoor life William adores. We own our motorhome. Our bills are a fraction of what they used to be. I've *never* felt so liberated. So free to be living and learning.

We started our small businesses, learning as we went. Yves began driver training, teaching George and his friendship group before word got out and he ended up with as many clients as he wanted. He also escorted large loads along the narrow Guernsey roads and we both covered security for a cannabis farm in Guernsey. With the advent of recognition that cannabis has a number of medical benefits, we both enjoyed being part of an industry that could redress the social injustice around the current drug policies.

I had retrained as a Coach, studied Reiki to stay aligned with what it means to live a good life, and found the simplicity utterly liberating. I learned about the power of Cacao in its original form to support anxiety and mood, amongst a number of other things. This business grew, and was portable so, as we moved, it moved with us.

I also learned to prepare food differently during COVID-19 and, between a new eating regime, a detox with nutritionist, Daniel White, and the addition of Cacao, William found a much calmer, more focused, and centred sense of self.

What's In Your Cup?

High Grade or Ceremonial Grade Cacao is one of the biggest secrets I uncovered.

Commercial chocolate, for many of us in the western world, undergoes an intensive process that includes roasting the Cacao beans at high temperatures. This alters the chemical composition and reduces many of the natural benefits found in Cacao. Have you ever been confused by the mixed reports of chocolate being good or bad for you?

As a consumer, I bought chocolate in a bar, with little thought to the processing or industry around it. I have noticed over time that the bars have become smaller, the sugar content higher, and the cacao content lower.

I now know that this is a heavily processed way of meeting a natural craving or need for chocolate. Minimally Processed Cacao, that is high grade or ceremonial grade, preserves its natural properties and health benefits, allowing us to receive what was always provided in the plant and bean, which is what our bodies actually seek. Minimally Processed beans are usually fermented and sun-dried, then ground into a paste or powder without being roasted at high temperatures.

This type of Cacao is pure, and it does not contain added sugars, dairy, or artificial ingredients. It's not overheated, conched, tempered, or altered in any way that degrades the dense nutrition this little bean provides.

It consists of one hundred percent Cacao, including both Cacao solids and cacao butter in their natural state, and retains a high content of antioxidants, vitamins, and minerals, as well as theobromine, which can have stimulating and mood-enhancing effects.

I was introduced to Cacao in a spiritual and ceremonial context by a person following indigenous cultures, who taught that Cacao was often consumed as a drink during rituals. It did not take long for me to feel better, ditch my excessive coffee use, and switch to including Cacao in my dietary choices.

In a very short time span, I recognised the health benefits in myself—no longer requiring antidepressants to manage what life was throwing at me. I understood that caffeine fueled my stress response in my central nervous system. Cacao worked with my cardiovascular system—I felt calm and peaceful, focused, and my mood was much improved—and I started to consider it as a natural support for William. We developed recipes together to find natural ways of supporting anxiety, from Banana Cacao smoothies, to Cacao homemade cereal. We added nut milk for creaminess and cinnamon in the autumn.

I explored Cacao, their regions for natural growth near the equator, and found a great fit for my family in Keith's Cacao. Our founder passed away early in

2024 and I regret never being able to sit on the porch in Guatemala with him. I met him online, and his spirit and resolve to reintroduce Cacao to share these incredible health benefits with a world consumed by coffee houses was a mission I was keen to be involved in, particularly as I continued to experience my own sincere transformation with this support. As I studied Cacao, I came to understand the added benefits of improving heart health, and providing a source of magnesium and other nutrients when in a high-grade form.

Over the last few years I have worked to bring Cacao to my community, with many people able to use it as an alternative to antidepressants and other prescribed medication. Unless you have a serious heart condition, Cacao is both superfood daily nutrition and support for your mood. Cacao offers significant support for feminine changes and assists in supporting focus and inspiration.

In more than one sense, I ask, "What's in your cup?"

It's not dark chocolate, it's a real hug in a mug. It's whole, pure, unadulterated Cacao.

A little bit of magic in a stress-fuelled world. (But only for people; it's highly toxic to pets.)

PART IV. LIFE ON THE ROAD

Travelling in the UK

OUR TRAVELS IN THE UK and onwards are available at our Facebook page *Adventures in Learning*[1] and in the first few months of this incredible adventure, we climbed the Three Peaks (Ben Nevis in Scotland, Scafell Pike in England, and Snowdon in Wales) and simply enjoyed each other, learning as we went.

> As a family, we redefined "learning" to be less of a "system by which a child is sat down and given instruction," to "creating spaces where discovery could take place, finding interests and inspiration."

We started our travels by visiting Scotland with George and leaving him, for the first time, at his prized university placement, The Royal Conservatoire of Scotland. The city was a big move from the smaller island life he was used to, so we travelled around Scotland for the first two to three months, staying close enough in case we were needed and far enough away to give him the independence he craved.

This is the new balance we needed to find with George, too. As our children age, parenting shifts from standing between our children and the world, to standing beside them, and then firmly behind them in their choices as they mature. As they develop skills, we encourage that independence by shifting to the side and allowing the wonderful opportunities to experience life and learn from mistakes.

Mistakes had been hammered into William as something to avoid—because he had learned that feelings of shame and worry came from making mistakes. Our systems have this wrong, and we wanted to make space for mistakes to

---

1. *Adventures in Learning* is our personal blog documenting our family's homeschooling journey through day-to-day stories, practical tips, and inspiring photos.

be nothing more than the learning experiences they are. Mistakes encourage knowledge of self and self-discipline.

Not allowing for mistakes only encourages fear and control.

In the workplace, I had repeatedly heard cries from the longer-serving employees, who just wanted the younger ones to "take the initiative" or "show initiative." Our existing system of education appeared to be discouraging this, probably unintentionally, as more and more rules and control were introduced. Would you feel encouraged to try something you were not sure would work if you knew you would be disciplined or shamed if something went wrong?

Over Christmas, we visited our extended family in the UK amid fears of Boris Johnson "locking down" the country and preventing families from seeing each other. It was a hard time for our family as we had chosen a new way of eating that they were not used to, and a new way of being well that did not accord with their belief that there was an absolute need to vaccinate us all.

One thing we had learned from the detoxification process was just how sensitive William's stomach was. Having achieved a balance, I was reluctant to upset it again and sought support from a local doctor in Guernsey in case we came into contact with COVID-19. He showed us another way and prescribed Ivermectin. This treatment was little discussed in the noise of vaccination coming through the airwaves and TV screens.

We carried on, COVID-free, throughout our travels.

Naturally, my parents were very worried and were not able to see all that we had worked so hard to achieve. They believed that vaccination was the only way to stay safe because they trusted, unreservedly, what they had been told. They were not being offered options, nor did they have to explore them.

This difference of ideologies started a rift.

We are the "strange" part of the family; we don't live nearby, and we're always "off doing our thing." I do appreciate that my family doesn't fully understand why we have felt the need to make these choices.

For many parents who embark on a home education journey, it's a hard fact that their extended family just wants them to keep trying to change the system. Their love can become lost in a fearful communication of not knowing what the future looks like.

Maybe our older generation see it as us "giving up." I understand that perception but I don't agree with it. I wasn't dying on a battlefield defending our rights, because no one recognised the battle we were fighting. Initially, we felt like an isolated voice in a large room where everyone else knew better. Once I realised I was on a battlefield, I needed to find my squad. No one had gathered us all and directed us to battle with a particular focus, so we were all fighting on our own little fronts. Standing back and realising that this was not going to change in a timely way that would benefit my child meant I needed to take action for him first. It's only now that I'm finding my squad and I realise we are not alone in this battle for change in seeking to address the fundamental way we view Education.

Others, like us, understand that the resistance to change the systems and processes that are not serving us is a relentless and overpowering struggle that, so far, we have faced individually. I would very much like us to come together with the greatest minds in education—Sir Ken Robinson, Zach Stein, Naomi Fisher and many others—who are trying to be heard as they speak for our children. They need the support and the stories of the parents to drive this change forward because governments are only seeing the expense and continuing to miss the mark.

It's unlikely that our children will see the benefits in their allocated school years, so withdrawing them and covering education ourselves until the changes are evident seems to be an entirely effective method to preserve and protect our young, whilst continuing to advocate for change. I have referenced some incredible change agents in this book and I invite anyone to consider their work as alternatives to our current systems.

Before leaving Guernsey, Yves and I were approached by a local business owner with a proposal. He visited our home several times, offered us directorships, and expressed a strong desire to work in partnership. He was seeking skilled employees to help with a new community venture focused on health and wellbeing. Despite his good intentions, many in the community were unhappy with him, and he was facing legal action. He felt this was unjust, as his goal was to benefit people's health and wellbeing.

I explained that we were leaving soon, but he was insistent that we would be of great help to him. After a brief period of volunteer work, the business owner asked Yves and me to continue working for him upon our return from our travels. We agreed, knowing that we could not be paid but he assured us that we would be paid as Directors later, as the business developed. We undertook a range of tasks, believing we were securing future income along with the idea of supporting the community with an affordable wellbeing centre.

Unfortunately, the business owner did not keep his word. As soon as I completed the immediate work for him, he asked us to leave. No remuneration at all. This experience was a valuable lesson in business: we could be as fair and reasonable as we liked, understand that people had no money to pay at the time, accept during the COVID-19 pandemic that accountants had not filed paperwork etc., but others might not share the same values. The idea of earning money with him—even at a later date—had, therefore, been squashed.

It may be recognised as sharp practice in business, but behaviour like this serves to erode trust. Fear is created if you are worried you will look foolish or get something wrong.

We were truly blessed in our friends though, one of whom put us up in her home without question and supported us fully and unconditionally. I will be forever grateful to her and her family.

During this time, we led by example in role modelling to our children that mistakes can happen, and can be painful, even costly. The learning that flowed from this was terrific. We had never been in business before and discovered new aspects to be aware of. For William, the lessons were more centred around the concept of discrimination. He perceived harm and watched his parents struggle. He was angry and saw the difference between us and the Indian family we had befriended and, with childlike innocence, wrote off an entire community in one sentence: "I don't like Indian people!"

Isolating it to the personalities of two people was a terrific lesson for him and the discussions were heartfelt and open, without any fear of reprisals or calls home to worry about the language he had used. He was free to explore his feelings and be understood and supported. He had a right to his anger at what had occurred, and to consider that a culture may be very different, and he needed to explore that in a safe and supported way until he understood that one person rarely represents an entire community, unless they are openly speaking for them.

Discussions followed about Nelson Mandela and other historical figures who represent communities that we have little experience of. Learning flowed.

Home Educating William

What is Home Education?

For our family, home education has offered a holistic approach to learning that perfectly matches William's unique needs. It allows us to create a curriculum that can be as structured or as flexible as we like, one that adapts to his interests, abilities, and developmental stages. This personalised method ensures that William receives an education appropriate to his age and ability, which has fostered a love for learning that was often stifled for him in traditional settings.

In our home education environment, learning is not confined to the walls of a classroom or the pages of a textbook. It doesn't have the structure of dictated lessons or learning at certain times, and plays more to the "What's he interested in today?" style of learning.

It integrates various aspects of life by turning everyday activities into valuable educational experiences. Whether it's a nature walk that doubles as a biology lesson, a cooking session that teaches maths and chemistry, or a trip to a museum that brings history to life, the opportunities for learning are limitless. They are natural and receive little resistance, unless William shows a clear lack of interest. It's OK for our kids to do that. I'm not interested in every little thing. If that changes later, I leave my need to learn it until then, and I've watched William embrace the same methods with ease. It makes me wonder at the value of grading children on subjects where they, as yet, have no real interest?

I also question how much we separate things out and compartmentalise learning in schools.

Could schools benefit from recognising that there is limited value in separated fields of study? These subjects have such a natural crossover with other fields that give a more holistic picture of the learning we are seeking.

Our approach in home education can vary from being curriculum-based, or following a set of educational guidelines and milestones, or it can be completely freeform; all of these allow William to explore subjects at his own pace.

The beauty of home education lies in its flexibility. If a structured curriculum worked best for our family, we would adhere to it closely, ensuring all necessary academic skills are covered. Conversely, if our child thrives in a less structured environment, we can take a more relaxed approach, focusing on experiential learning and curiosity-driven exploration. He even has days where he wants to see what I'm doing on the computer, what he can help with, and how things work in the world of business. As I learn, he learns.

William was inspired to write while watching me engrossed in my own healing by writing a journal and blog posts. He wrote his own story, that became a short book, that became a series of books, exploring feelings of growing older, new experiences, and his interest in mythology and sites of ancient history.

Home education also respects and nurtures William's individual learning style. We have observed that he learns eagerly through hands-on activities when he is inspired, and we tailor his education to suit this need. By understanding how William learns most effectively, we can provide him with the resources and opportunities that align with his natural curiosity.

Moreover, home education allows for a pace that is just right for William. He can spend more time mastering difficult concepts without the pressure of keeping up with a class, or he can move ahead in areas where he excels, fostering a sense of accomplishment and confidence. This adaptability ensures that learning remains engaging and appropriately challenging.

For our family, home education is about providing William with a space that meets him where he is, nurtures his natural curiosity, and prepares him for a lifetime of learning.

It's an approach that values the whole child by respecting his individual pace along with his individuality. It respects his right to be interested in what interests him. He has gone on to create a rich, diverse, and deeply personal educational experience. Our hope is that he will develop a love of learning for life, rather than think he is finished when school is out.

Part V. Big Dreams and Aspirations

Vision for Change

W<small>E HAVE MET OTHER</small> home educating families, as you can imagine, and crafted a whole new address book of contacts in the areas of progressive education.

My business and news feeds contain complaint after complaint from parents isolated by diagnosis or "unacceptable behaviours." On many occasions, these behaviours are simply communication of frustration, of not being heard, or of not having their needs recognised and valued. If these children are unable to access essential services, suspensions and exclusions follow. Wider groups are emerging in support of this need for change in how we view education.

Also evident are the fears and worries of the elders in our community who have placed their trust in the idea that education involves, or comes from, a school. I do have compassion for how hard it is for an entire generation of school attendees to have their children reject the environment they knew.

Whilst there have been many changes within education in the last fifty-to-seventy years, the idea that these changes are not serving the children and grandchildren of this generation, or may be contributing to the poor mental health and wellbeing of our younger generation, is difficult for many of our elders to comprehend.

Our elders have been led to believe that our children should attend school to learn effectively. They do not recognise any disempowerment of the parent. They are exposed to mainstream news and media talking about the breakdown in family values, and miss that each time we gave away our trust to the systems, we disempowered the family. More recent years have given further worries with sanctions and efforts to threaten children and parents who are not complying with school attendance, which have only added to these fears. We are not regularly provided with news that explains where this system has limits, nor have we adequately questioned why these rules and limits are, in fact, necessary.

Greater minds than mine are working on the problem, and I recommend anyone considering the changing needs in education to look into the work of Sir Ken Robinson and his manifesto *Imagine If: Creating a Future for Us All* (Robinson 2022).

For further reading on how children best learn, we are equally guided by Clinical Psychologist, Naomi Fisher[1], who gives a strong voice of reason in questioning why we educate via schools that do not first consider how children best learn.

In *Education in a Time Between Worlds,* Zak Stein powerfully suggests that our world is currently undergoing major transformation, and that the subjects taught in schools are becoming irrelevant at faster and faster rates (Stein 2019). He suggests that human development and learning must be understood as our most valuable resource—and speaks clearly into the flaws of standardised testing.

Ultimately, our current system is cheap. It meets the needs of some children, but that does not make it fit for all.

With the advent of technological advances, Education has now been made more available to adults and children alike. Charities and innovative teachers who leave school buildings to teach online provide outstanding support for children to direct their learning towards subjects they have interest in. Outside the known world of school is a world of readily available learning and research. Support is offered in many of our communities for young people to identify their interests in the fields of sports and culture. Home and travel exchanges are taking place amongst many worldschooling or home education families. We can access courses online that cater to a wider variety of interests than the average school curriculum.

---

1. Dr. Naomi Fisher is a clinical psychologist, author, and speaker. Her Facebook page provides insights into home education and self-directed learning approaches.

As an added bonus for families, this way of learning online is highly portable which makes travel for families possible outside the school holidays—and the elevated premiums that accompany them.

Are we at the point where we can trust that children have valid ideas about what they are interested in?

World Cruise Adventure

Home education groups and support networks are springing up everywhere, with parents finding each other over social media and community channels, sharing the pain of their children not fitting the system and collaborating on progressive projects that invite us to consider other ways of learning. Within these networks, William has discovered niche groups with shared interests. He works on his social skills with an already identified interest, which in turn seems to make it easier for him to access his personality, rather than learning to adapt to others' needs and wonder why he is miserable.

In 2023, we travelled away from our motorhome to explore the idea of further travel and learning about different cultures that interested our son at the time. We recognised William was far more comfortable and had progressed from needing to travel with a familiar space to being curious about the world around him. In January 2024, we invested a sizable chunk of our pension and embarked on a world cruise, something I could only have dreamed of in my working life and equally something many of my peers hoped to do "once they retired."

The educational value of such a journey may seem obvious at first, but there were surprising outcomes of considerable benefit that I had not appreciated when we made the booking. Of course there would be the introduction of different cultures and lands, and an exploration of history and geography. I had not, however, considered the community that would grow around us in the shape of the people we shared our journey with.

In reflection, it's probably no surprise that I did not give much thought to other travellers on this grand adventure. Our family had bonded closely in our learned understanding of where William was, and focused solely on his needs. At that time he had no interest in socialising at all. His school-based peer group had left him with many questions and he was comfortable with withdrawing. In many ways, we withdrew too.

Shortly after boarding, however, we discovered excited travellers with places they wished to see and explore. In these people, we discovered a community of onboard elders who were eager to share their wisdom. Many of them were natural teachers, while others were former primary and secondary teachers. William discovered them simply by standing out, as he was frequently the only child on board.

As our journey continued, he became friends with these elders and surprised Yves and I when he asked us to step back a little and let him attend games and events on his own. He found that when we were there, he became the "child of us," rather than having his own "friends." On sea days, I watched him take ownership of his explorations, establishing what events, lectures, and games were offered on the timetable. It encouraged me to see him find the confidence to talk about the games they were playing, and to plan and prepare for his day. He made arrangements to meet people at lunchtimes, asked what excursions they were enjoying, and was curious about what they saw and if it was different to him. He soaked it up. William established a firm rapport with the table tennis crowd, the curling and carpet bowls teams, and the darts and shuffleboard players. He found board games again, and discovered real joy in ballroom dancing. This anxious boy also took to the theatre stage, in front of a crowd of hundreds, to share his joy in this "talent" with his community at an impromptu talent show. He made friends for life as this group of elders followed his journey of learning and eagerly waited to see which interest grabbed him next.

He learned to sew and made a toy.

He joined a team and built a boat in a challenge set by the crew.

He explored the crew and their work, attended cooking demonstrations, and visited the bridge of the rather fabulous ship we were experiencing. We chose a ship with a smaller volume of people on board so he would not be completely overwhelmed, and he found joy in it all. The captain and crew were beyond marvellous.

He learned to manage unexpected change when a third of our cruise was altered, due to conflict in an area of Israel that meant places he was looking forward to seeing could not be safely accessed.

He experienced different financial systems and worked maths with money exchanges.

In just three-and-a-half-months, he went from feeling like the unteachable and unwelcome child to anyone who was not his parent, to being seen as: "A fine young man." "What a credit to you he is." "What a remarkable and polite young man he is." A joy for his community to be around.

His wounds were visibly healing. As were mine.

Part VI. Settling and Growth

William's Development

As I write, William is thirteen-years-old and showing significant development. Gone is the angry and upset child who no longer wants to live because he feels he does not "fit" or belong with his peers.

After three years away from a traditional school environment, he has had time to discover himself. William recognised that he didn't like to be around large numbers of children—and that's OK.

After the cruise, he decided he was ready to try being with kids again, and started to meet with those with shared interests. He understands that his interests are not necessarily shared by people of the same age alone. It's strange to me that society even chose to group children this way; that their age was the determining factor for sharing a space rather than anything like a shared interest. It's a hangover from a time when our children left school to enter industry, which required children to be of a certain age and skills base. Whilst our industry has changed significantly in two hundred years, our methods of education have remained grouped by age. I also notice the overarching expectations of particular developmental milestones being reached by certain ages, rather than allowing the stages to develop in the order that feel more natural for the child.

During our cruise we met many different elders with a huge range of skills and abilities. I have always known this valuable resource was there, but it is not generally encouraged in our busy world. Like a terrific library of experiences and knowledge walking the decks, William gravitated to his interests and found ways to engage and play as he learned. His curiosity was met with a high degree of tolerance, encouragement, patience, and understanding. The education went both ways between the parties at times, as William helped them gain a better understanding of technology and mobile phones. Now, our family belongs to a wider community of people who are all learning as we go.

Home Education does not require you to recreate school at home. It's trusting your child to find their own passion and interests, and guiding and supporting them through these discoveries. It can simply be offering a range of opportunities to them to see what they like, and if one is established, you can explore it together.

From Scouts and sports to board gaming, William works from areas he is interested in to develop socialising in his peer group. He has found other home educated children around the world and connects with them online.

Our learning space changes, as he needs it to, from in-person and hands-on learning to online and subject research learning and socialisation. He has significant autonomy around his own learning and I've not found any handicap in this. Over time, he has developed interests in a wide range of subjects. Some—such as ancient history, writing, and geography—we recognise as being present in the traditional school curriculum. Many other subjects, like astrology, geology, and mythology, would not appear on the curriculum of a traditionally-schooled teenager.

William, like many children his age, loves to play. Sometimes he wants to play badminton and in-person games with his friends. Sometimes he goes through phases of wanting to be alone and use his computer and games. There has been so much anxiety caused for parents whose children enjoy computer games, again without much context.

We are taught that screen time should be limited, should only be age appropriate, that blue light causes sleep disturbances, and all the fear that goes with screen use. It's a "bad" parent who leaves their child to explore the world of tech.

We rarely recognise the social understanding and online safety that can come with playing in this way. For many children, being one step removed from the communicator is vastly more manageable than those who only know personal socialisation. It's a balance.

Online, kids are playing, creating, socialising, and working through problems together. As part of a worldschooling community, William works collaboratively with children around the world to provide safe gaming server access. He was motivated to resolve issues with another student and I'm watching them work together to resolve challenges and issues for their community. I am aware of the predators, and so is he.

We have a few boundaries around screen use, phones, computers, as well as TV, that help to support being in a good relationship with them but, ultimately, we value the learning that is coming from the wider, progressive education and gaming community.

Once we managed the anxiety by recognising and validating it, we found ways to work with it. The first way was entirely natural and was addressed by rebalancing the gut with his diet (GAPS - see References). The second way was to add a high grade Cacao to his menu options to help reduce his anxiety.

As mentioned earlier, the term "high grade" or "ceremonial grade" Cacao is not the same as chocolate. These terms refer to different products derived from Cacao beans; they differ from regular products in their processing, composition, and intended use. Most chocolate is so far removed from Cacao as to be unrecognisable in its benefits.

Notably, William sleeps well, lives well, and is a happy child who is working to understand his environment and his place in it. As he becomes more settled, his curiosity grows in relation to the world around him, which he now understands is a far larger and more diverse place than a playground of school allows for at his age. He prefers to socialise across age groups.

The Data Protection Development

Having decided to draw a line under all that happened with the Guernsey services, Yves and I left the matter behind. It was far too complex, intertwined, and from education services specifically, it was incomplete. We could not unpick it all, alone, when we needed to focus on our son. But we did draft a letter outlining our enquiries and disagreement with the accuracy and the content of the information.

It's important for us all to be aware that our personal data is kept by many services and it follows us wherever we go. Any information on record stays on record and, as such, it's important it's correct. Like checking your credit rating and ensuring that data is accurate, it's advisable to see how authorities have been recording data about you and your child/ren. You can ask to see it because this data held about you belongs to you too. In legal terms, it's relatively new to a lot of the services. As a result, they are learning to be open to these checks, and you will be amazed at the gossip and rubbish recorded there as the services come to grips with recording data properly.

Given we already had a "heads-up" that it wasn't accurate—right in front of us at the educational meetings—the letter we drafted highlighted all of these inaccuracies, along with the others on file. Our letter was given to the Office of the Data Protection Commissioner. We exercised our right to challenge the information on file and also ensured any data shared from that point onwards was shared in a way that notified the recipient that we had questioned the accuracy of the data at the earliest stages. This letter was to accompany any onward disclosures that may become necessary.

Services need to share information to serve us, but many need your permission and it's helpful to let them know if you have issues with the data. This was agreed by all to be a reasonable solution in complex circumstances that involved multiple agencies. The alternative was to pay for an advocate, which our budget would not stretch to at the time. Justice has become expensive to families seeking redress, especially in Guernsey, where I could be paying upwards of hundreds of pounds an hour, in a case likely to take several months to unpick.

The covering letter however, advised anyone receiving this information that there were potential difficulties with it and to treat it with caution. These difficulties were acknowledged by the services too, which helped. It was the best we felt we could do, and afford, at the time.

Upon moving to the UK all our records and documents had to be transferred which, we were informed, had occurred without incident.

In late 2023, I had cause to access medical records to provide information to our new local services regarding William. Medical records carry one of the highest standards of confidentiality regarding protection of your personal data. During that process, I found an active flag that suggested William remained the subject of child protection in Guernsey.

Sick to my stomach, I had to start the process again, gathering all the records that had been shared to ensure they were complete.

They were not. A sizable portion of the records were missing and there was no trace of our letter. I was forced to make contact again with Data Protection Officers to establish why this had occurred.

The government services in Guernsey initially insisted that they had shared all information and smeared our GP practice as people who had failed in their duty of care to us. I was assured that this was nothing to do with the States of Guernsey.

I duly followed their insistence and made enquiries with my former doctors' surgery in Guernsey, who then provided me with a letter to return to the States of Guernsey department, clarifying that they had received no information from the authority. The States of Guernsey were then unable to evidence their position that they had shared everything as required, despite their earlier insistence.

We have been asked to accept a further apology.

They assure me "lessons have been learned" and that they now have a more robust system in place that evidences what they have shared and what they have not. This system was in place before I left Guernsey and just was not used.

In the words of Charlie Brown, "Good Grief."

The office of the Data Protection Commissioner has been notified and replied that they are not minded to investigate.

We can appeal if we wish.

Part VII. Conclusion

Reflections and Future

WHEN REFLECTING ON OUR transformation so far, several crucial lessons emerge. From an early age, we are taught to measure and compare ourselves to others, often without questioning the systems that enforce these standards. Our experiences have highlighted the complexity of these systems and the necessity of challenging them to find better paths forward. Change, as we've learned, happens gradually, and just as our personal transformations didn't occur overnight, neither will the systemic changes needed in education.

I am concerned that the governance of state schools, in the UK specifically, are only considered to offer increasingly disciplined and harsh conditions to our children and their families. We know of schools that encourage children to be dragged into school for "registration"—in their pyjamas if necessary—just to get the child through the door. These schools show no awareness of *why* increasing numbers of children are resisting being in school.

The pressure on schools to improve attendance without addressing the underlying causes has led to a troubling trend of conflict between parents and educators, often to the detriment of the child's well-being. This situation is not unique to the UK; it is a global issue that reveals the systemic flaws in how we approach education.

Are we suffering needlessly, when leading educators like Sir Ken Robinson and the creative mind of Zachary Stein have been imagining education differently for some time now? Clinical Psychologist Naomi Fisher, and Peter Grey, a Research Professor of Psychology[1], both outline that many children learn best naturally and through play—so why are we abandoning these methods? We've discovered that there are always alternative ways of approaching challenges;

---

1. Gray, Peter. *Free to Learn: Why Unleashing the Instinct to Play Will Make Our Children Happier, More Self-Reliant, and Better Students for Life*. New York: Basic Books, 2013

ways that may not be immediately apparent but can lead to surprising and meaningful outcomes when we remain open-minded. This openness, paired with a willingness to question the status quo, is essential as we consider the needs of our children and their families as a whole unit.

Our journey into home education has shown us that many families share similar struggles with the school system often exacerbating, rather than alleviating stress in an effort to control a desired outcome. These experiences underscore the urgent need for a more compassionate and individualised approach to education, one that genuinely listens to and respects the needs of children and their families. Most child welfare laws reflect this and I struggle to comprehend why our system of education does not.

It is crucial that we, as parents, take back our role in guiding our children's learning, and question whether traditional schooling is truly the best fit for them. This may involve exploring alternative educational methods that align more closely with our children's unique interests and needs. This, however, requires support from schools and authorities, rather than the adversarial stance many parents encounter.

Ultimately, the power of choice—both for parents and children—is vital in education. We must advocate for systems that value individuality, creativity, and well-being, that parallel academic achievement focused establishments and value these areas as highly. Rigid conformity is not capturing the hearts of minds of our youth. As we face the challenges of change, we must remember that we have the ability to question, learn, and choose paths that best serve our children's futures. In doing so, we can help shape a more humane, varied and responsive educational system.

As for me, it took me time to consider the question: "Does my child *need* to be in school?" I had no knowledge of other methods of learning, but I knew I learned quite well on my own initiative, and with people I chose to collaborate with.

It took me time to discover that there was, in fact, a law in place that enables a parent's discretion regarding school attendance, and that to withdraw a child from school was entirely possible. I simply had to deregister him.

I became aware that local authorities also differ in their approaches and there are some stories and parent experiences where there has been considerable input and judgement on what an education in the home should look like when you deregister, or choose not to register, your child.

My child questioned *everything,* as do many others—why certain shoes need to be worn rather than those that are comfortable, the value of a uniform, starting school at the time it starts, homework, the punishment and reward system, the study of subjects as mandatory—when they are at stages where these subjects don't capture their attention and they just want to play. They question the force with what is happening. They question the need for it. They question why it is so regimented.

In these moments, I believe the damage of such a metric lies in that the child is led to believe there is some deficiency in them for not having an interest or ability at the age that some arbitrary person suggested they might. If they have a different sleep pattern, a different eating need, the urge to go to the toilet at inconvenient times or frequencies, their "difference" is highlighted in a negative light.

If the status quo remains, our schools will continue to value only one type of intelligence above all others, when our communities need a mix of all the different types of intelligence to thrive. As a system, education has not established how to measure the humanity in our children. It's not quantifiable. I recently found an online school that is challenging itself to improve this by measuring the sense of wellbeing each child had in attending. Change is coming, but it's not government-led or freely available.

The Power of "Or"

Mental health in our children, and for many parents, is at an all-time low.

I did not think there could be anything in my values and beliefs about education and learning that would cause such a clash with teachers. It left me flummoxed for some time.

> *No one is supposed to "fit" at the expense of who they are. Whoever they are, wherever their interests lie, there is value.*

Until a system values the range of human interest and ability, it will always fall short in its ability to assess value. Can any teacher, hand on heart, state they are encouraged to value art and singing in the same way as mathematical achievement?

As we favour systems over learning, we handicap teachers and children, and incapacitate them from finding a love for who they are and what interests them. We do not need "one size fits all" in this—we need variety and to speak to the opportunities for education and development of skills for lifelong learning. Let's face it, learning and growth never stops.

A library of knowledge could go further than books.

The Human Library[2], an international organisation and movement that first started in Denmark, uses a library analogy—but it lends people rather than books. The Human Library's intention is to provide a way to meet people you would not otherwise perhaps meet, in the ordinary course of your life, so gaining the opportunity to ask questions and learn directly from them.

Can we apply this variation to schools with this theme of a library of people who want to share their knowledge? Imagine teachers who love their subject being

---

2. Human Library. "The Human Library." Accessed October 31, 2024. humanlibrary.org

accessible to those of any age who desire to explore it? There are many people outside government, education departments, and schools, who are redesigning and considering how we provide, access, and serve children in education.[3]

Is it possible now to grasp these ideas and reconnect our children with a love of learning?

I have a vision where our existing schools become these libraries—human libraries of spaces where teachers who love their subject can just be available, on a published timetable, to any student who wants to learn what they know. No exams, no tests for teachers or pupils—just an exchange of knowledge with times for introduction and times for supportive ongoing exploration. We've got the teachers, and the spaces, but with so much structure in place, there is no imagination allowed on either side.

Imagine a world where schools transform into vibrant human libraries—spaces fueled by passion and curiosity, where teachers are available to share their knowledge with eager learners. Picture students exploring freely, diving into subjects they love without the constraints of exams or rigid curricula.

This dream can become a reality, but we need your voice to make it happen! Challenge the conventional structure that stifles creativity and imagination in education. Advocate for a system that values the exchange of knowledge over standardised testing.

Take Action Now:

1. Share Your Vision: Talk to your friends, family, and community about the potential of schools as human libraries. See what the blocks are and work to overcome them within your community.

---

[3] Progressive Education. "Progressive Education." Accessed 2023. progressiveeducation.org

2. Engage Educators: Connect with teachers who are passionate about this approach and encourage them to join the conversation.

3. Use Your Voice: Write to local education authorities, attend school board meetings, and advocate for a more flexible, student-centred learning environment.

4. Spread the Word: Use social media to share this vision and inspire others to join the movement for educational transformation.

Let's unleash creativity from those boring school buildings and create a future where learning knows no boundaries. Together, we can turn this dream into reality! Will you take the first step?

We can access many courses online at organisations such as Outschool and the Khan Academy, and many other educational resources, but it's also true that not all children learn well this way.

Can we admit we have this horribly wrong, not just for neurodivergence, but for any child whose interest falls outside an increasingly narrow curriculum with stringent controls?

How can we encourage creativity, change and innovation if a learning environment is not flexible enough to meet that?

When I reflect on our transition, I see there has been real discovery, innovation, and change for us as a family, simply from hearing William and discovering what he needs.

There has been a transition many would label "magical" as a result of both our children not fitting this system, in their individual ways. With the right support flowing to him, one of my boys was able to establish himself within the system, yet the other received harsh judgement, punishment, and exclusion far too young. The damage caused by this is taking considerable time to unpick.

By not "fitting" in his way, George showed us the value of standing firm to support our children in their choices, despite more regular careers being encouraged for reasons of financial safety. That safety is an illusion, as many government and career workers will tell you. George had fabulous support in his school, and at home, and was able to trust and work with his adult guides who valued him and gave him room to be who he is.

By not "fitting" in his way, William showed us the limits of our current system of education. It was horrific to have experienced the lack of trust and manipulation we were faced with, and it's taken me a few years to investigate and challenge this for myself.

Teachers are stuck. They are not encouraged to innovate, and in some schools, the words and actions really do not match. In an effort to "tick boxes" and "fit" into the system themselves, they have been forced to manipulate—the lowest vibration of leadership skills on the agenda. They have been forced here by the upper tier they answer to, who themselves often have little comprehension of the severity and impact of the education system. They show this by continuing to instil rules and force in this system, punishing consequences that are handed out to schools, that go on to punish teachers, who go on to punish and restrict pupils. It's systemic, and has created a tendency to distort.

Justice and Health

Our government educational systems are not alone in this. Justice and policing has done the same thing. Rather than work to reflect the community they serve, lead by example, and focus on high quality service, they have not been able to measure the human factors and only measure crime, punishment results, and what is written. They, too, distort facts and figures to misrepresent our communities as fearful places to live. They have made a decisive move away from "service" to "force." No wonder they have lost the community trust in Guernsey.

Justice is a system that they have been playing with for too long—understaffed, undertrained, and undervalued as much as teachers are. Health care staff, too. The message to them all from their upper tier is clear: We do not value your experiences. It does not fit with our agenda.

Many new officers are not trained or encouraged to develop and use their discretion to serve their community. Instead, officers are required to consider and follow the policy. Discipline within the service is now about following policy as much as it is following the law. It's an unhelpful approach to replace valuable training, and does not encourage any compassion or growth alongside the community. Community is stronger when officers reflect their community, are a big part of it, and serve their members with compassion. Force was always the last resort. Why, then, are they now a Force?

Health, as I have touched on, has similar issues. Health Services contend with "Fabricated and Induced Illness (FII)" policies that are not dissimilar to those we experienced in education.

On 14 November 2023, Cerebra published the findings of a major research project concerning FII. This research report considers the prevalence and impact on families in England, Scotland, and Wales of being accused of creating or exaggerating their child's difficulties—an extreme form of parent carer blame. Instances of this kind are referred to as "Fabricated or Induced Illness" *(Cerebra 2020)*.[4]

The major finding of the research is one of family trauma. Fifty percent of allegations of FII were made after a parent carer had complained about the actions of the relevant public body.

Is this the same kind of knee jerk defence of the system that we faced? Parent carers save the government almost unquantifiable amounts of money each

---

4. Cerebra. *Fabricated or Induced Illness Research Report*. 2020.

year. By becoming the experts in their children, they save government costs across the board in additional staff and specialised training *(Green 2020)*.[5] Yet the average government allowance for these parent carers falls way below the minimum wage. Many parents, like us, are forced out of strong professional backgrounds because of a lack of service support, to take on the role of parent carers, which involves a huge salary drop, new training, no support, and full responsibility.

But the health and care systems are littered with staff who wish to serve from the start of their employment as healers; who wish to support community wellbeing; who know that being separated into body parts is not looking after the whole person. Or the whole child. Or the whole family. We have lost sight of unity and I wonder if that started by seeing ourselves as parts?

A person cannot enjoy health if the mind is sick and tired. The mind needs to rest.

A person cannot enjoy health if the body is injured or experiencing pain. It needs time to recover.

A person's spirit is an essential part of who we each are. When the spirit is broken, it needs time to heal.

Instead, we are told to medicate—because it's faster. It's faster to prescribe an antidepressant or drug in many cases than to access specialised care or therapy.

It's also cheaper.

Suppressing feelings of distress and outrage that at some point need to come out is not conducive to overall well being.

I have heard the phrase emphasising that it takes a community to raise a child.

---

5. Green, Will. "Unpaid Carers Save States £29m a Year." *Guernsey Press*, August 13, 2020.

We cannot be a community if we are divided into so many parts.

My spirit was broken by a combination of all of the above.

With time, I am healing. I'm finding my way back to a body I am comfortable in, with my food carefully chosen out of aisle upon aisle of products that offer speed over health as nourishment. Nutrition is a fundamental part of our health, and whilst all doctors and nurses know this, how often are they encouraged to sacrifice their own good nutrition in favour of speed to manage the long and arduous shifts they work? The hypocrisy is evident in having a message for the patient about healthy living, all while being in a system actively working against natural health. Long shifts, poor rest, lack of outside spaces and fast-food choices because the breaks are short, is how the system works with its staff, all the while advocating the opposite to patients.

The systems we have come to rely on also remove our sovereignty and right to refuse. This is evident especially at a young age in our children's schools. We are not looking at *why* they are saying "No." We are forcing them in.

We encourage and value speed and force over service to the community and that is being demonstrated, often without much challenge, in each of our services.

We are also in a time of change.

Which direction will you take?

Epilogue

Looking Forward

We will continue our journey as a family, learning as we go. We stand ready to share our discoveries with all who need that support, and to continue to serve our community with talks, podcasts, and blogs that remind us all that we are our child's first hero.

It is my hope that our story will support anyone feeling alone or powerless, and provide a light at the end of any difficult tunnel.

Deciding to home educate has been both challenging—and liberating.

To the extended families:

I understand it's different and scary when your child makes this choice for your grandchildren, nieces, and nephews. You don't want life to be difficult for anyone. There have been so many rules built up about schools, attendance, and teachers' struggles, that we have forgotten to question the "one size fits all" idea.

The grandmothers and grandfathers we have met in other communities are the wisdom keepers and the "glue" that made communities possible. The children accessed the elders who held the knowledge that they were passionate about and, in this environment, learning simply flowed. You are a key part in it and if you can trust that, it's the biggest support you can offer.

To the partners and parents:

Find each other. Come together, create and imagine together, and grow the places our children want to learn in so we don't have to force them into places they cannot be.

To the siblings of the change agents:

We thank you sincerely for your patience with these little people who need something just a bit different. You are better placed to understand and manage change than anyone else I know. That's a powerful space to occupy, and I trust you will know exactly how it integrates as we all move forward. Lead us.

And to our change agent children:

We need you. Thank you.

Questions

I had questions and continue to seek the answers I need.

I've compiled a list of the questions I had and where I found further information in case this shortcuts the effort for you tired parents and carers.

Does my child have to go to school?

The answer here depends on where you live. Germany does not allow home education, but many other countries have a section of the Law that requires a child to receive an education in a school or otherwise. It's this "otherwise" that covers a wide range of educational options—some are recognised schools such as Montessori or Steiner Schools, which you may find entirely appropriate for your child. There are also the online schools, like The School Beyond Limitations, and dip-in-dip-out services of many providers, such as Outschool and Khan Academy.

So first, check the law where you live. You can access information online, via your education department, Citizens Advice, or free legal services that are offered by many law firms for the first half hour.

Check social media for groups in your area and charities that are set up to answer common questions. I have also discovered help from the volunteer sector in relation to support in negotiating with schools about flexible schooling.

Why is school the way it is?

Further information is available from the legendary Sir Ken Robinson—check out his TED talks and read *Imagine If*. He is an inspiration. His daughter, Kate, collaborated with him and continues to work on educational revolution.

Changing Our Minds by Dr Naomi Fisher is an amazing read for how we learn and why we school our children. She is all the power you need in your corner for considering alternative education. She offers webinars and collaborates with change leaders and parents alike to offer support with all things neurodivergence.

Take a deep dive into unpicking connecting systems and get a look at possible futures with Zachary Stein, either online or through his published works.

How do I travel on a budget with my children?

Everyone's financial circumstances are different, but a host of alternatives are growing quickly, known as "Education Otherwise" in a nod to the phrasing in the very law in Guernsey that advises that Home Education is acceptable. These changes in offering are worth keeping an eye on. It's true we may all be in the same storm, but our boats look different. Through my business, Gemini Directions, for example, I coach families considering home education to help them find clarity in the choices that they wish to make and the steps to get there.

You can find many offerings online to suit most budgets for formal learning if that suits you and your child. The beauty of this is that formal learning travels with you. You can even find private schools that offer flexible classrooms online, e.g., The School Beyond Limitations.

Our story of changing our finances may inspire similarly positioned people. Living in a motorhome may appeal to others (it's worth paying out for one that offers good insulation in winter if you want to travel full time!) Simply joining Home Education communities, or looking for house swaps in other countries, or working abroad with accommodation provided, are all options for travel with children. It's cheaper than school holiday travel too.

What is the difference between home schooling and home education?

They are completely different terms each with their description of how education in the home can look.

Home Schooling: This offers a system of learning similar to a school, involving programmes of study but from the child's home environment. Some children find academic study appealing; the routine and focus is fine, but the school environment is not conducive to their needs. They may take exams (private entrance) in all, or some, subjects, and they progress at their own speed.

Home schooling does not have to be six-plus hours of study a day. Many families factor in a few hours on a one-to-one basis with their child, and achieve what teachers need a full day to explore with many children.

The cost of materials, study aids, and exams are borne by the parents with no support from authorities, but it's possible to consider exploring funding for your child in the form of sponsorship. I know a child who had no regular exams, but passed all accountancy papers, and some firms will consider paying for these exams. Many companies are looking for specific skills and if that's a natural interest for your child it's possible they may consider supporting you.

Home Education: This is a term used to describe a natural way of learning life skills, and tends to be led by the child looking to learn a specific interest. It recognises that learning is always happening as an organic thing being part of a family or group.

Home education is not about structure, although it may have some regular events of interest to the child. We moved from starting school from home for a few hours each day, to project-based learning that specifically interested William, to joining clubs and events of interest to a more home educated, almost "unschooling" type of home education.

What is Unschooling?

Unschooling is when a child deregisters from school. When a child no longer goes to school there is a transitional period for them, and their families, where they take the time to adjust to what education from inside the home may look like. Education may simply continue this way, where a child leads their learning needs and interests, and as they are identified, the parents, peer group, and community support the child in their discoveries. It's a holistic way of learning, where subjects and experiences blend.

Few children like to sit down for all their learning, but many like to use a calculator to add up the shopping. We once played a game of "the floor is lava," and my son spontaneously wanted to place his times tables on furniture and pillows. It was led by him and his wish to know. Whilst there was a structure to times tables, he found a spontaneous interest in knowing what they were.

Is home education a barrier to higher education?

Simply put, No. Your child may choose to access higher education by taking traditional exams and applying through traditionally recognised channels, or to take an access course in the subject of their interest. There are a number of guides online and from local authorities about taking exams as a home educating family.

Many universities will guide and advise what they will consider for particular courses of study, some will offer placements for particular courses with evidence of outside achievement in the subject area, others will interview for a place and some subjects will require entrance exams.

In *Changing Our Minds*, Naomi Fisher explores studies that you may find supportive in these enquiries. It's worth remembering that universities are likely to be impacted by the changing landscape of education, and their entrance requirements may well change with it.

References

"Almost Two-Thirds of Unpaid Carers Took on Role Due to No Other Options – Report." *Guernsey Press*, June 9, 2024. guernseypress.com/news/uk-news/2024/06/09/almost-two-thirds-of-unpaid-carers-took-on-role-due-to-no-other-options--report

Cerebra. *Fabricated or Induced Illness Research Report*. 2020. cerebra.org.uk/research/fabricated-or-induced-illness-research-report

Green, Will. "Unpaid Carers Save States £29m a Year." *Guernsey Press*, August 13, 2020. guernseypress.com/news/2020/08/13/unpaid-carers-save-states-29m-a-year

Paton, Graeme. "Special Needs Used as a Cover for Poor Parenting." *The Telegraph*, May 4, 2012. telegraph.co.uk/education/educationnews/9246067/Special-needs-used-as-a-cover-for-poor-parenting.html

Rethinking Education

Talks and Further Reading

Fisher, Naomi. *Changing Our Minds: How Children Can Take Control of Their Own Learning*. London: Robinson, 2021

Georgia. "Why Autism Is Much More than an Excuse, and Why It Matters." *Mind the Flap*, February 17, 2018. mindtheflap.wordpress.com/2018/02/17/why-autism-is-much-more-than-an-excuse-and-why-it-matters

Gray, Peter. *Free to Learn: Why Unleashing the Instinct to Play Will Make Our Children Happier, More Self-Reliant, and Better Students for Life*. New York: Basic Books, 2013

Human Library. "The Human Library." Accessed October 31, 2024. humanlibrary.org

Progressive Education. "Progressive Education." Accessed 2023. progressiveeducation.org

Robinson, Sir Ken. *Changing Education Paradigms*. Filmed October 2010 at TED. TED video, 11:41. ted.com/talks/sir_ken_robinson_changing_education_paradigms

Robinson, Sir Ken. *Do Schools Kill Creativity?* Filmed February 2006 at TED. TED video, 19:24 ted.com/talks/sir_ken_robinson_do_schools_kill_creativity

Robinson, Sir Ken. *Imagine If: Creating a Future for Us All*. London: Penguin, 2022

Robinson, Sir Ken. *The Element: How Finding Your Passion Changes Everything*. New York: Viking Penguin, 2009

Stein, Zachary. *Education in a Time Between Worlds: Essays on the Future of Schools, Technology, and Society*. Santa Barbara, CA: Bright Alliance, 2019

Stein, Zachary. "Zachary Stein: Education, Development, and Philosophy." Accessed 2023 zakstein.org

Facebook Resources

Neurodivergence

PDA Parenting
The *PDA Parenting* page provides community support for PDA parenting approaches.
facebook.com/pdaparentinguk

Missing the Mark
Missing the Mark is a blog about parenting neurodivergent children and spreading awareness on the PDA profile.
facebook.com/MissingTheMark1

Sunshine Support
The *Sunshine Support* Facebook page is an award winning Special Educational Needs & Disabilities (SEND) Consultancy that provides resources and advocacy for families navigating educational and support services.
facebook.com/SunshineSupportUK

Home Education

Dr. Naomi Fisher
Dr. Naomi Fisher is a clinical psychologist, author, and speaker. Her Facebook page provides insights into home education and self-directed learning approaches facebook.com/drnaomifisher

Human Design

Karen Curry Parker
Discover your Life Purpose and unique energy blueprint with Karen, Founder and Creator of the Quantum Human Design™ for Everyone Training System and the Quantum Alignment System™
facebook.com/KarenCurryParker

Nutrition and ASD/Aspergers/ADHD

Gut and Psychology Syndrome | GAPS Diet
Dr. Campbell-McBride gained a Postgraduate Degree in Neurology and developed her theories on the relationship between neurological disorders and nutrition. She completed a second Postgraduate Degree in Human Nutrition and is one of the world's leading experts in treating children and adults with learning disabilities and other mental disorders, as well as children and adults with digestive and immune disorders.
facebook.com/GAPSDiet

Keith's Cacao
The *Keith's Cacao* Facebook page shares information on cacao's health benefits and ceremonial uses. facebook.com/keithscacao

Cacao Recipes
This space of Tory's is set aside for seasonal recipes and ideas for all things Cacao. facebook.com/groups/1533427157127745

Podcasts for Further Exploration

Accepting the Unacceptable: Parenting Autism, Epilepsy, Special Needs. Podbean.
The *Accepting the Unacceptable: Parenting Autism, Epilepsy, Special Needs* podcast series provides insights and support for parents navigating special needs challenges. podbean.com/podcast-detail/hihaw-8e82a/Accepting-The-Unacceptable-Parenting-Autism-Epilepsy-Special-Needs-Podcast

Enjoying Home Education. Podbean.
The *Enjoying Home Education* podcast offers over 300 episodes covering topics that support research and practical advice for home educators, with insights applicable beyond the U.S. context. podbean.com/pu/pbblog-jnrjg-30f9e2

Hands Around The Globe Podcast
Join Tiffany Cameron and Tory for "mum talk" about special needs parenting, school, healing, and community. handsaroundtheglobe.org

Home Education Matters. Podbean.
The *Home Education Matters* podcast offers valuable discussions and resources for supporting home-educated children in the UK and beyond. podbean.com/pu/pbblog-rt54k-e86675

Locked up Living. Podbean.
The *Locked up Living* podcast provides insights into the realities and challenges of institutional environments. podbean.com/pu/pbblog-cnivz-9eef21

"Dr. Naomi Fisher on Schools and Compliance in Education." *Locked up Living.* Released March 23, 2023. In this episode of *Locked up Living*, Dr. Naomi Fisher discusses school compliance and the impacts of mandatory attendance on children. podbean.com/ew/pb-wwr69-131eb6c

Stark Raving Dad
The *Stark Raving Dad* blog and podcast offers resources and support for homeschooling parents, focusing on the joys and challenges of home education starkravingdadblog.comstarkravingdadblog.com/tag/podcast

Podcasts for Children

My Friend Autism. Podbean.
The *My Friend Autism* podcast episode explores personal experiences and offers valuable perspectives and insights related to autism. myfriendautism.podbean.com

Who Smarted? – Educational Podcast for Kids. Podbean.
The *Who Smarted?* podcast offers educational content for children on a variety of topics in an engaging, kid-friendly format.

Big Life Kids Podcast. Podbean.
The *Big Life Kids Podcast* provides motivational stories and lessons to help kids build resilience and a growth mindset
podbean.com/podcast-detail/a5agh-8fa81/Big-Life-Kids-Podcast

Home Education: Learning Resources for Kids

Outschool outschool.com/

Centre of Excellence centreofexcellence.com/

Khan Academy khanacademy.org/

Ted Ed Kids ted.com/playlists/702/ted_podcast_kids_and_family

Other Resources

Adventures in Learning
Adventures in Learning is our personal blog documenting our family's home-schooling journey through day to day stories, practical tips, and inspiring photos. We share our hands-on, interest-led approach to home education, with activities ranging from outdoor exploration and science experiments to creative arts, reading, and projects. Each post offers actionable ideas and insight into nurturing a love for learning at home, ideal for families looking to personalise their educational journey.
facebook.com/profile.php?id=100076296610686

Gemini Directions
Whether you are buying Cacao, looking for safe spaces to gather with other parents, courses or our podcasts come and find your community here. Gemini Directions is growing and changing to accommodate all the ways things become possible. If you cant find what you need, message me.
geminidirections.co.uk

National Autistic Society
Search here for your local branch, courses, and other resources. autism.org.uk

Autism Guernsey
If you'd like to learn more about autism, and keep up-to-date with the charity's latest news for Guernsey. autismguernsey.org.gg

The Decider Skills
The Decider Skills uses Cognitive Behaviour Therapy to teach children, young people and adults the skills to recognise their own thoughts, feelings, and behaviours, enabling them to monitor and manage their own emotions and mental health.
thedecider.org.uk

Montessori Schools
goodschoolsguide.co.uk/choosing-a-school/alternative-schools/montessori

Steiner Schools
goodschoolsguide.co.uk/choosing-a-school/alternative-schools/steiner-waldorf

The School Beyond Limitations
school-beyond-limitations.com

Acknowledgements

Our sincere and heartfelt thanks go to:

National Autistic Society (Guernsey) Branch and Autism Guernsey for all the support in our most troubled times. We would have felt very lost without your kindness, knowledge and experience.

Everyone involved with Keith's Cacao, for the education, the space holding, and the daily blessings you bring.

The professional people breaking ranks and finding a better way for our children—the teachers, social workers, police officers, medical workers, clinical psychologists, parents and carers and charities supporting them all. You are not responsible for the system staying as it is and give us hope with your courage to find a better way.

To the parents hearing their children and taking the time to sincerely explore if the same way is really the best way.

To Kristina and her team at Captured by KC Designs for the graphic design and illustrations.

And for Ruth. My powers of manifestation must have been at an all time high when I found you. Our story begins here with our little bit of Magic.

About the Author

Founder of Gemini Directions and Co-founder of Adventures in Learning, Tory Lenormand is a passionate Mother, Coach, Cacao Practitioner, and Author who champions family, well-being, and community. She believes in empowering others to explore their needs, question long-standing practices, and develop thoughtful perspectives that align with a greater sense of purpose and balance.

Tory understands that one size does not fit all for our communities. Following her years of experience as a police officer and financial investigator, she learned to embrace difference whilst becoming a keen observer of how government services increasingly rely on threat and force as a quick fix for deeper issues.

Having witnessed with dismay children being pulled into school in their pyjamas, teachers unable to manage competing needs of children, and parents feeling increasingly powerless against the growing control of this system, she offers her book, *The Magic Of Not Fitting In*, to review these patterns and question oppressive conduct. Tory encourages others to reconsider what they believe is possible.

As a Cacao Practitioner, she shares this old plant medicine to support her family and the wider community. She strives to promote balanced well-being for everyone, particularly our children.

With both her sons, Tory has experienced the joys and challenges of different educational paths. Her oldest son thrived in a traditional school environment, while her youngest, diagnosed with Autism Spectrum Disorder (ASD), faced difficulties in that setting. This led Tory to embrace home as the primary space for her youngest son's education, creating a nurturing and supportive learning environment tailored to his needs. Tory's parenting and education philosophy focuses on equipping children with practical tools to thrive, and counters the pressures of high-speed living whilst fostering a sustainable, supportive legacy where children feel seen and heard.

Governments don't change the things we need. People do.

www.ingramcontent.com/pod-product-compliance
Lightning Source LLC
Chambersburg PA
CBHW052143070526
44585CB00017B/1957